Indian Tribes
of the
Northern Rockies

Also by Adolf & Beverly Hungry Wolf:

"Children of the Sun"
"Shadows of the Buffalo"
"The Ways of My Grandmothers"
"The Blood People"
"Siksika"
"The Blackfoot People"
"Charlo's People"
"The Good Medicine Books"
"Rails in the Canadian Rockies"
"Off on a Wild Caboose Chase"
and other titles

Stoney Encampment, 1971 (AHW Photo)

INDIAN TRIBES
of the
NORTHERN ROCKIES

Compiled By
Adolf & Beverly Hungry Wolf

BOOK PUBLISHING COMPANY
Summertown, TN
USA

GOOD
MEDICINE
BOOKS
Skookumchuck, B.C.
Canada

PREFACE

The main purpose of this book is to present a volume of cultural information and historical facts about several neighboring tribes living in and around the Rocky Mountains of British Columbia, Alberta and Montana. It is especially intended as a handy reference for younger members of those tribes, who see a lot of educational material about the rest of the world, but not so much about their own.

A second purpose is to provide important and interesting historical material about these tribes to the general public, to encourage better understanding and greater respect towards the native people of this land.

The heritage of these tribes is much too great and complicated to cover in a single book, especially one of this size. Readers are encouraged to seek out volumes listed in the bibliographies for further study and information.

Book Publishing Company
P.O. Box 99, Summertown, Tn 38483

ISBN 0-913990-74-4

Canadian ISBN 0-920698-11-5
Published in Canada by
Good Medicine Books
Box 844, Skookumchuck, B.C. Canada V0B 2E0

Hungry Wolf, Adolf.
    Indian tribes of the Northern Rockies / complied by Adolf & Beverly Hungry Wolf.
        p.   cm.
Originally published in 1989 by Good Medicine Books.
Includes bibliographical references.
ISBN 0-913990-74-4 : $9.95
1. Indians of North American--Rocky Mountains--Social life and customs. 2. Indians of North America Rocky Mountains--History. 3. Indians of North America--Canadian Rockies (B.C. and Alta.)--Social life and customs. 4. Indians of North America--Canadian Rockies (B.C. and Alta.)--History.   I. Hungry Wolf, Beverly. II. Title.
E78.R63H86 1991
971.1--dc20   91-17796
                                                                                  CIP

CONTENTS

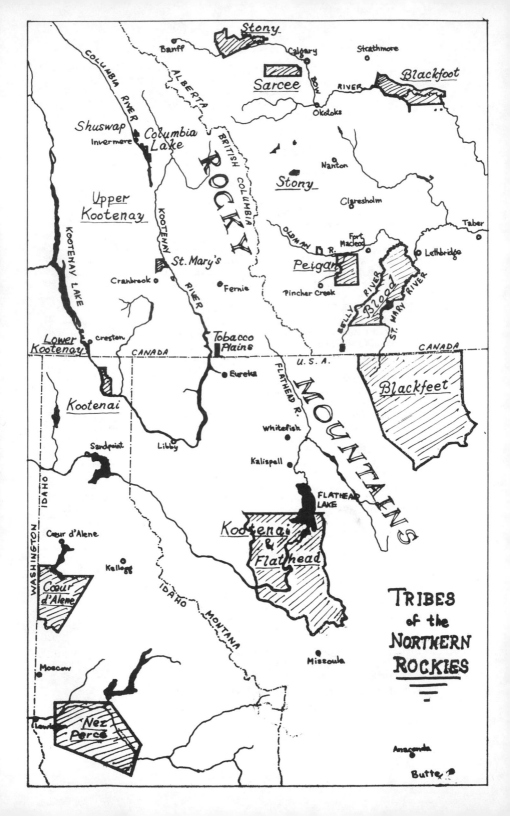

INTRODUCTION

Just over one hundred years ago, the thousands of native people of the Northern Rockies still lived in tipis, hunting and roaming after herds of buffalo. They were masters of a vast terrain covering parts of today's Alberta, British Columbia, Idaho and Montana. Included in this country are three of the world's most famous national parks, Banff, Jasper and Glacier, mighty mountains, rivers and lakes as well as vast stretches of grassy prairies.

The largest and most powerful of these tribes was the Blackfoot Confederacy, made up of four distinct groups who usually lived apart, but kept in constant contact with each other for strength and security. Their many warrior societies consisted of thousands of well-armed men, many of whom made pledges to stand and die in the face of enemies, if their people were threatened.

Bands of the four Blackfoot divisions could be found anywhere between the Red Deer River of central Alberta and the Yellowstone, deep down in Montana; from the peaks of the Rockies, eastward across the plains into Saskatchewan and eastern Montana. The Old Man River, Chief Mountain, and the Sweetgrass Hills are just three of the famous landmarks that feature prominently in ancient Blackfoot legends.

When Blackfoot camps were in the area of today's Calgary, they were probably not far from their Sarcee friends and allies, who spent a lot of time in that area of the Bow River, within easy reach of the mountains.

Living and hunting even closer to the mountains were the Stoneys, who still roam some of the same crags in which their forefathers sought mountain goats and mountain sheep. Travelling in small groups, they preferred to camp and hunt in the Rocky Mountain foothill country, which they roamed between Montana's Glacier National Park and the area of present-day Jasper.

Across the mountains from the Stoney's live the Kootenays, who used some of the same trails, so that the two were often friends, and trading partners. The former Kootenay range of lakes, rivers and beautiful valleys in British Columbia still carries their name. Their southern relatives live on the U.S. side, where the name is spelled Kootenai and Kutenai, though either way the people all consider the boundary line an intrusion upon their ancient territory.

At the south end of Kootenay country begins the equally splendid Flathead range, home of the mis-named Flathead people, who are distant relatives of the Pacific Coast Salish. At one time they occupied both the Mission Valley and the Bitterroot, though now they only live in the former. Like their Kootenay neighbors, they made seasonal excursions to regular campgrounds across the mountains on the prairies, where they replenished their supplies of buffalo meat and hides.

Although each tribe claimed its own territory, all five were neighbors, so that they saw each other often. Sometimes their meetings were friendly, other times they led to war. More often they raided each other in the nights, usually for women and horses, though especially for the challenges and adventures, plus the social honours they brought.

While they lost individual fights and battles with each other, it is important to understand that not one of these groups was ever beaten as a tribe. None ever lost a battle, nor tasted the humility of defeat. This fact has helped these people to maintain a fierce pride in their tribal heritage, even after more than 100 years of less violent but also ruthless social and psychological conquest by the greatly outnumbering non-native population.

No one can deny that federal troops could have destroyed these tribes by sheer force of numbers, had North American governments behaved like many other invading forces around the world. It would have been a costly victory - all five tribes were known for having brave and dedicated warriors, who knew well their wildly rugged battlegrounds. North American history could have turned out quite differently, just in these Rocky Mountains, alone.

Instead of risking these great losses, both federal governments approached the native people of the Northern Rockies with offers of treaties - promises of friendship and other benefits - if the natives would allow non-natives to come into the land without fighting. The two sides had vastly different ways of looking at life, but the native people understood the treaties to say something like this:

"Thanks for letting us Europeans take over most of your hunting and camping lands without war. In return for your peaceful agreement, we'll be your friends and share some of the proceeds with you and your descendants. Also, we'll let you people carry on with your basic tribal life, undisturbed, as long as you stay on the small pieces of lands reserved for you forever. Besides that, we'll send equipment, supplies and teachers to help you learn our ways, too." To the native people that sounded like the best of both worlds.

Since that long-ago time when those treaties were made, a succession of non-native governments have tried to redefine those treaties to suit their own ends. This has led to much frustration and resentments among the native people. Their culture had no writings; peace treaties were made by sharing the smoke from a pipe and making sacred verbal oaths, which must then never be broken. The native people accepted written treaties on the understanding that they were the same as sacred oaths. To make sure, they also shared pipe smoke with the treaty bringers.

All the tribes in this book feel that they have not received what the treaties originally promised them. They are especially bitter because their part of the transactions were settled long ago, when they gave up the lands. It is important for you to know this, as you begin to read this book, for it is a major theme of their contemporary life.

Because this book is mainly concerned with history and culture, some readers might think people of these tribes still live in tipis, or at least in places out of the way from the rest of society. Actually, another volume like this could easily be filled with modern-day stories and statistics. The membership of all five tribes has grown and developed tremendously in recent decades, with great strides forward in education and economic self-sufficiency. In planning the future, it helps to understand and be proud of the past.

Stoney rider in Banff National Park, c. 1950
(Canadian Pacific Photo by Nicholas Morant)

ABOVE: A group of Blackfoot boys, their faces painted, during initiations for a warrior society, c. 1890. (C.W. Mathers Photo)

Blackfoot Origins

The Blackfoot Confederacy consists of four divisions who speak the same language, are well intermarried, and share a common tribal heritage. Back in the Buffalo days, Blackfoot people were proud hunters and nomads who developed a rich and spiritual culture as part of their Life in Harmony with Nature. Today, they are among North America's most progressive Indian tribes, with modern education and skills having profound impact and causing tremendous social changes, yet the people have managed to keep alive many cultural traditions left from their tribal past.

The four divisions could once have been a single tribe, perhaps known by the name Blackfoot, but no stories about this have been handed down. Blackfoot history depended on oral records—the language was never written—until explorers first came and began writing things down in the late 1700s. Since that time, many stories and legends have been recorded from chiefs, medicine people, and other wise elders. According to them, the Confederacy came to the Buffalo Plains from a forested country further North.

Hundreds, or even thousands, of years ago the Blackfoot people might have been part of a larger group that included the Gros Ventres, Cheyennes and Araphahoes. All of them share what is called the Algonkian family of languages, with distinctly different roots from many other tribes, although widely spread across North America.

One ancient legend that these Algonkian-speaking people, including the Blackfeet, have in common concerns the crossing of a frozen body of water, which broke open at that time, dividing the people into two large groups, permanently. The ice break is said to have been caused by an old woman, following her grandchild's request to pull up a buffalo horn frozen into the trail. Some believe this was in the middle of a river, breaking up two Indian tribes, while others believe this refers to the frozen Bering Strait, and recalls when Algonkian ancestors supposedly came to North America from Asia.

Whatever scientific theories say about ancient migrations, Blackfoot elders agree that all people originate from the same source: *Ish-tsihuy-dabeeope*, or The Creator. From this source comes all life; to explain some of the details, there are numerous Blackfoot myths comparable to stories in the Bible.

The leading character in Blackfoot mythology is Napi, or Old Man, who represented the Creator here, on Earth. Some say he was the Creator's servant; others tell how he and a brother were children of the Creator's first two people, a man and woman who had trouble involving an evil, magical snake. At any rate, Napi had lots of magical powers of his own, with which he sometimes helped the people, at other times tricked them. His tales of adventure were prime entertainment at Blackfoot campfires since earliest times.

Some say that the people were first called Blackfeet because of dark soil they walked through in their Northern forest land, before moving out on the Plains. Others say the name comes from wandering over burnt prairies in search of Buffalo. As far back as legends tell, only one of the four Blackfoot divisions has actually called itself *Siksikah*, or Black Feet. The others have only become known that way in the English language, though all four now proclaim themselves proudly as "Members of the Blackfoot Confederacy."

Alexander Henry, one of the first white visitors to the Blackfeet, wrote in 1810, "They are the most independent and happy people of all the tribes East of the Rocky Mountains. War, women, horses and buffalo are their delights, and all these they have at command."

The Four Blackfoot Divisions

1. *SIKSIKAH* — The actual "Blackfeet," sometimes called "Northern Blackfeet," or the "Canadian Blackfoot." The Blackfoot Reserve lies East of Calgary, Alberta, and includes the towns of Gleichen and Cluny.

2. *KAINAH* — meaning "Many Chiefs," though better known as the Blood Tribe of Alberta. Their reserve, the largest in Canada, lies near Waterton National Park, and includes the town of Stand Off.

3. *PIKUNNI* — meaning "rough-tanned robes," pronounced "Pay-gann" in English. The *Ah-but-ochsi-Pikunni*, or North Peigans (spelled *ei* in Canada) are neighbours of the Bloods, with a reserve located between Fort Macleod and Crowsnest Pass, including the town of Brocket.

4. *PIKUNNI* — same as above, but *Amskapi-Pikunni*, or South Piegans (spelled *ie* in the U.S.), now officially known as the Blackfeet Tribe of Montana, located on a large reservation between the Rocky Mountain foothills of Glacier National Park and the former Buffalo plains, including the towns and communities of Browning, Heart Butte, Starr School, Babb, St. Mary and East Glacier. The two groups of Pikunni separated completely in the early 1800s, after a fight between two men over a woman, although very close ties remain today.

Blackfoot Camp - 1883 (Photo by C.W. Mathers)

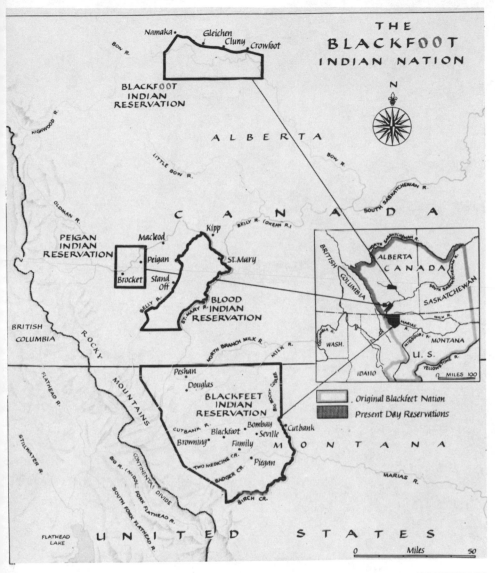

(From Walter McClintock, THE OLD NORTH TRAIL)

4

Mountain chief - Warrior, leader and historian of the Pikunni - Blackfeet, 1909.
(Rodman Wannamaker Photo)

Mountain Chief's Winter Count

An Indian History Covering 61 Years of the Blackfoot Confederacy
Obtained from Mountain Chief at Browning in 1911

1. The fall of the year, Gambler went on the warpath and was killed. Piegan spent the winter on the Marias River. (This was the year 1850.)

2. In the fall of the year, Big-lake, chief of The-Don't-Laugh band died; Piegan wintered on the Marias River, which was high and flooded their camps. In the summer, they had a sun dance at Sweet Grass Hills; Bob-tail-horse was shot and killed; a woman was also killed.

3. Leaves-big-lodge-campmarks clubbed a Flathead but did not kill him; in the summer, Piegan killed some Sioux on the Marias.

4. Black-tattoo became crazy; in the spring a man named Goose was killed by Sioux; in the summer, Goose's father went to war and killed some Crow; some of the Crow escaped by letting themselves down a high cliff with a rope.

5. Still-smoking was killed; the Piegan stole a sorrel race horse from the Flathead. In the summer some Piegan were on the warpath south of the Missouri River. They came to some white settlers and there saw a Sioux Indian whom Last-bull killed with a club. The Sioux had been visiting with the white men.

6. In the fall, the first treaty was made by the Government at the mouth of the Yellow River; there were seven different tribes there. That winter, Mountain-chief spent on Belly River. The clothes of one of his daughters caught fire and she was burnt to death. During the summer Mountain-chief became ill with the hiccoughs which lasted some time.

7. This winter was called the slippery winter because there was so much ice. In the summer Mountain-chief and his people went to Canada and killed thirty Sioux.

8. The Piegan camped on Marias, and one by the name of Blood killed a Flathead Indian. Lame-bull, a chief, was killed by falling from his horse in the summer.

9. Mountain-chief spent the winter on Milk River and found an extra large buffalo dung which was about three feet across when measured. Chief Big-snake was killed in the summer.

10. Lazy-boy was killed. In the summer, the Blood camped at Yellow Mountains and fought among themselves; Calf-shirt killed some of his own people.

11. A man named Peace-maker was killed. Eagle-child was killed in the summer; a Blood was shot through the face with an arrow by a Sioux but did not die.

12. Piegan fought with the Gros Ventre and one, Many-butterfly, was killed. The Piegan killed five Sioux, who had a horn spoon.

13. Chief Coward was killed by Crow Indians. In the summer, the Piegan attacked the camps of the Gros Ventre and killed many of them; also, some Piegan were killed while out hunting.

14. The Assiniboine attacked Mountain-chief's camps on Big River in Canada, at night, but did not kill anyone. The Piegan fought with the Gros Ventre in the summer and a Piegan, whose name was Half-breed, was killed.

15. Piegan had what was called red smallpox; in the summer they attacked the Assiniboine's seventy lodges and running them out captured the lodges.

16. At Fort Benton, the Government gave the Piegan clothes, etc.; the white man who issued the things to them went by the name of Black-horse-owner. At this place they also made peace with the Gros Ventre. In the summer Little-dog was killed

and the Piegan fought with a great number of enemies, with the Crow, Assiniboine, and Gros Ventre who helped one another in fighting the Piegan; but the Piegan overpowered or whipped them all.

17. Bear-chief was killed south of the Missouri and the following summer the Piegan killed Weasel-horse, a chief of the Blood.

18. Mountain-chief camped south of the Missouri and the Piegan killed two Flathead near the Piegan camps; in the summer the Piegan killed thirty Assiniboine who were picking gum off the pine trees.

19. Strangle-wolf was killed by the Gros Ventre while out hunting; Chief Crow was killed by Gros Ventre while he was out hunting. He had six women with him.

20. The Piegan had smallpox and the soldiers attacked seventy camps, killing many old men, women and children. Running-raven was wounded by a Gros Ventre.

21. The Piegan fought with the Cree on Belly River in Canada and killed one hundred of them. In the summer they had a big battle with the Assiniboine and Big-brave and his horse were wounded.

22. A Piegan, Red-old-man, was killed by the Gros Ventre near Bear Paw Mountain while he was trying to steal some horses from them; Black-eagle, a Piegan, killed an Assiniboine and his wife, in the summer.

23. Bull-chief and High-wolf died; while they were on the warpath in the summer, White-man's horse and his war party were nearly all killed.

24. Calf-chief killed two Flathead Indians near the Piegan camps while they were about to steal some horses. Black-eagle was killed by the Northern Blackfoot in the summer.

25. The Agent issued hogs' heads to the Piegan as rations; in the summer Big-nose took four Assiniboine prisoners.

26. There were plenty of buffalo and many Assiniboine came to visit the Piegan. In the summer the Agent, known as Wood, issued clothing, etc., and the Piegan made peace with the Crow at Sweet Grass Hill.

27. A Piegan killed his wife who was a Sarcee woman; in the summer, Chief Calf-chief died.

28. Open winter, there was no snow all winter; Big-buffalo-rock died during the summer.

29. Weasel-moccasin was killed by the Assiniboine; had a sun dance; cattle tongues were first used for sun dance; Agency was moved down where it now is.

30. Piegan moved and camped south of the Missouri; in the summer the soldiers brought the Piegan back to the Reservation.

31. The Piegan wintered south of the Missouri; Black-cheek was killed by the Flathead, In the summer, the Piegan moved back to the reservation and an Indian was accidentally shot by the Agency doctor during the sun dance.

38. White-dog, an Assiniboine, was killed by the Piegan; Big-brave and many others lived on Birch Creek seven winters and summers.

39. In the summer Big-brave moved to Blacktail Creek and wintered there.

40. Mares were issued to the people and Little-dog received two buckskin mares.

42. Big-brave moved to White Tail Creek and lived there two winters and summers.

61. Big-brave moved to Blacktail and has been living there ever since, nineteen winters and summers he has lived there.

Big Spring illustrates the old way of recording Blackfoot events and history.

Glacier National Park, 1913

White Man's History of the Blackfoot Confederacy

1730 First horses seen by Blackfeet, being ridden by Shoshoni warriors. First guns also seen, used by Crees and Assiniboines. Arrival of first trade goods, such as glass beads and metal arrowheads.

1780 Hudson's Bay Company builds Buckingham House along the Saskatchewan River; first trading post close to Blackfoot country.

1781 Smallpox epidemic strikes Blackfoot camps for first time; over half the population dies! The disease was picked up when Blackfoot warriors raided a very sick Shoshoni camp, not knowing anything about the disease. This occurred in the Bow River country, which surviving Shoshonis afterwards left to the Blackfeet.

1784 The North West Company of independent fur traders and trappers moves into Blackfoot country to compete with the Hudson's Bay Company. Guns, knives, axes and arrowheads began replacing primitive weapons. Blankets, materials, pots and awls helped to make tribal household life easier. Tobacco, beads and paints became the first luxury items.

1787 David Thompson, of the Hudson's Bay Company, becomes the first trader to winter with the Blackfeet (Piegans), along Bow river. All these early trade encounters took place in Canada.

1794 Economy: 14 Beaver pelts = 1 trade gun.

                 1 Beaver pelt = 20 rounds of shot, with powder.

               30 Beaver pelts = "1 large keg Blackfoot rum,"

               made by mixing 4 or 5 quarts of pure alcohol

               with about 7 gallons of water.

1799 Rocky Mountain House built by North West Company, west of Edmonton, Alberta, becoming main Blackfoot trading center for some years.

1806 Piegans meet part of Lewis & Clark expedition in their territory, now in Montana. Fight breaks out and one Piegan is killed, starting out bad relationship between Blackfeet and American white men.

1809 Economy: 1 common horse = 1 gal. keg of "Blackfoot rum,"

               2 fathoms of twist tobacco, 20 balls with powder,

               1 awl, 1 scalper, 1 fleshing knife, 1 gun worm,

               1 P.C. glass, 1 fire steel, and 1 flint.

Richest Piegan in that year said to own 300 horses.

Population Estimate:

	Lodges	Warriors	Persons
Piegan	350	700	2,800
Siksika	200	520	1,600
Kainah	100	200	800

1815 A 17-year-old boy from Montreal named Hugh Monroe becomes the first "white Blackfoot," marrying the daughter of a Piegan chief and learning the life of her people. He remained with the Blackfeet, near Browning, until his death in 1896, being survived by many descendants.

1819 "Coughing" epidemic — one third die.

1821 Missouri Fur Company sends American trappers into Blackfoot country for furs. Piegans resent their intrusion, saying they stole the furs and traded guns to enemies, besides. A large war party annihilates most of the trappers in an ambush before the first year is through.

1823 Population Estimate: Siksika—500 lodges. Blood—300 lodges.

                            Piegans—550 lodges. Total — 10,800 persons.

1831 James Kipp, of the American Fur Company, befriends the Blackfeet and offers to trade for their fur, rather than sending trappers out after it. They agree to let him build Fort Piegan, on the Missouri River, in their territory. The first few days of trade brought in 6,450 pounds of beaver, which his company sold for $46,000. The Bloods didn't like it, so they burned the post down after trading season was finished.

1832 Blood head chief Bull's-Back-Fat brings the first delegation of his people to big Fort Union, in Assiniboine country, where they make peace with that tribe.

George Catlin becomes the first white artist to paint Blackfeet, calling them "perhaps the most powerful tribe of Indians on the continent."

Catlin's Population estimates: Siksika, 450 lodges. Bloods, 450 lodges. Piegans, 500 lodges. Small Robes (then largest band within Piegans), 250 lodges. Total of 1,650 lodges, with 5 to 10 people per lodge.

1833 German Prince Maximilian spends late summer with the Blackfeet to see how they live. Estimates Confederacy population at 18,000 to 20,000 people. The Prince, and his artist companion Karl Bodmer, are witness to an immense battle between Piegans and some 500 Cree and Assiniboine warriors, ending previous year's peace. Piegans eventually win the fight, though with heavy losses.

1835 Blackfeet bring 9,000 buffalo robes to trade at new Fort McKenzie, 32 days' travel by boat, upriver, from Fort Union, at the junction of the Missouri and Marias rivers.

1837 Smallpox again strikes the Blackfeet, arriving with infected people and clothing aboard a steamboat. Two thirds of the Confederacy is said to have died.

In spite of the sickness, over 10,000 buffalo robes were brought in for trade the next winter.

A frontier journal from that year notes that forty to fifty independent trappers were being killed in Blackfoot country each year.

1841 Blackfeet brought in 21,000 robes for trade. Some Indian hunters become eager for trade goods and start killing buffalo for hides. Professional white hunters kill even greater numbers of buffalo, mainly for tongues and hides.

In this year, Father DeSmet baptized first Blackfeet to Christianity.

1844 Good relations between Blackfeet and traders break off after smaller troubles lead one trader to fire a cannon into an innocent group of Piegans, killing ten and wounding others.

1845 Another smallpox epidemic strikes the Blackfeet.

1846 Fifty families of Small Robes band of Piegans wiped out by Crow attack, ending this group's often-independent journeys, sometimes in company of the Flathead tribe.

Blackfeet bring another 21,000 buffalo robes to trade, this time to new Fort Lewis, near the later Fort Benton. Head trader is Alexander Culbertson, a respectable man married to Medicine Snake Woman, the daughter of a Blood head chief and the sister of Seen-from-Afar.

1847 Alexander Culbertson moves Fort Lewis three miles down and across the Missouri River, renaming it Fort Benton. This becomes the most important trading center in Montana. Supplies travel 2,415 miles upriver by steamboat, from St. Louis.

Economy: 1 buffalo robe = 25 loads of ammunition, a gallon kettle, three knives, or 1½ yds. of calico.

3 robes = 2½ point wool blanket.

10 robes = 1 trade gun (for which traders paid about $4 back East).

10

1853 Observers on the Plains wrote that the "quantity of buffalo" was "almost unbelievable," and that "the entire country of the Blackfoot" was "perhaps the best Buffalo Country in the N.W."

Gov. I.I. Stevens meets head men of Blackfoot Confederacy, on behalf of U.S. Government, and proposes a great peace council to end wars among tribes, and to guarantee peace between Blackfeet and whites. Chiefs agree to council.

First photos of Blackfeet taken by artist John Mix Stanley, travelling with Gov. Stevens. Said to have been mostly portraits of chiefs, which were later buried with them; none of the photos survive.

Stevens' party also makes first "scientific studies" of Blackfoot country, recording plants, wildlife, minerals, geography, and details of Indian life.

Population Estimates:

	Lodges	Persons	Warriors
Blood	270	2,430	810
Siksika —	290	2,600	870
South Piegan ...	200	1,800	600
North Piegan ...	90	800	270

1855 "Lame Bull Treaty," signed by 26 principal chiefs of the Blackfoot Confederacy, defines tribal territories and proclaims peace between the tribes and the U.S. Government.

This Treaty council was the first important intertribal gathering in Blackfoot country, involving 59 chiefs and leaders from eight different tribes.

"Major" Edwin A.C. Hatch (all Indian agents were given the honorary title of Major) becomes the first Blackfoot agent, with an office at Fort Benton.

1856 "Major" Hatch writes first "annual report" on the Blackfeet for the U.S. Government, although he only sees them for four of his nine months on the job. Wrote that he gave out treaty annuities to "about 8,000 Indians," being members of all four Blackfoot divisions.

1857 "Major" A.J. Vaughan becomes second Blackfoot agent, and the only one for many years who had a good relationship with the people. A fur trader described him as follows: "A jovial old fellow, who had a very fine paunch for brandy, and, when he could not get brandy, would take almost anything else which would make him drunk. He was one who remained most of his time with his Indians, but what accounts for that is the fact that he had a pretty young squaw for a wife..."

1858 Agent Vaughan wisely recommends government prohibition of trade in buffalo robes, to prevent senseless slaughter of the animals. The suggestion is ignored by everyone.

1859 Jesuits build first mission in American Blackfoot country, St. Peter's, near Choteau, Montana. Indians show some interest in these unusual spiritual ways, but they are still 100 percent devoted to their own faith. Missionaries have plans to wipe out the old Indian ways, while Indians only want Christian prayers as added blessings to what they already have. Father Lacombe is first missionary among Canadian Blackfeet, having arrived in 1855.

Agent Vaughan supervises first Blackfoot "farm," which has limited success. Piegan head chief Little Dog tries gamely to set an example for his people with a small farm of his own, nearby. Interest drops when the Indians realize farms can't be brought along on buffalo hunts. Little Dog abandons his in favor of the buffalo, and his nomadic people.

11

1861 Long-time alliance between Blackfeet and Gros Ventres ends when enemy group steals horses from Gros Ventres and leaves some at a Piegan camp, leading Gros Ventres to think the Piegans stole them.

1862 Montana Gold Rush brings illegal miners across Plains to foothills of the Rockies, well into hunting grounds reserved for Blackfeet by 1855 Treaty. Miners are often among worst type of white men, along with some trappers, traders, and agents. Small, bloody encounters become frequent.

1863 Blackfeet see neither agent nor annuities promised by 1855 Treaty. New agent arrives at very end of year, describes Blackfeet as "degraded savages." Things get worse in Blackfoot country, and liquor flows more freely.

1864 Scarlet fever kills an estimated 1,000 Blackfeet.

1865 U.S. Government persuades a small group of leaders from Blackfoot Confederacy to sign a later-unratified Treaty reducing official Blackfoot country by well over two thousand square miles, in return for about one million dollars (today the price for a good ranch in this region!).

Blackfeet and whites murder each other, even within Fort Benton. Governor of Montana fears war is imminent and helps plan military action against the Blackfeet, who spoil things by moving North into Canada.

1866 American whiskey traders driven out of Montana into lawless Alberta area, where they build Fort Stand Off and other liquor posts, increasing the region's problems.

North Piegan war party burns down Blackfoot agency farm on Sun River. Nearby Jesuit mission is abandoned.

Head chief Little Dog, and son, murdered by drunken Piegans, near Fort Benton, for being too friendly with whites.

Economy: 1 buffalo robe = 2 tin cups of whiskey.
             1 fast horse = 4 gallons of whiskey.

1867 Fort Shaw, on Sun River, becomes first U.S. Army post in Blackfoot country, near new Blackfoot agency.

1869 Another Smallpox epidemic kills 2,000 Blackfeet.

Popular Montana rancher Malcolm Clarke is killed by relatives of his Blackfoot wife, leading to cries for revenge.

1870 Major Baker leads large cavalry force from Fort Shaw to arrest the killers of Clarke. In the depths of winter they attack the wrong Piegan camp and kill 173 people, mostly women and children. The only armed conflict between Blackfeet and U.S. troops becomes known as the Baker Massacre.

Last large intertribal battle takes place near Lethbridge, Alberta, when Cree and Assiniboine forces attack a Blood camp on the Belly River, not realizing that angry and well-armed Piegan "refugees" from the Montana troubles are camped nearby. That mistake cost the attackers between 200 and 300 men.

Population Estimates: Siksika = 226 lodges. Bloods = 212 lodges.
                     Piegan = 330 lodges. Total = 6,144 persons.

1871 U.S. Congress declares end of treaty-making with Indian tribes and nations.

Ranchers begin raising cattle along Sun River, claiming the Blackfeet have too much land.

1873 U.S. Government arbitrarily moves Southern boundary of Blackfoot country North by 200 miles, throwing open a huge piece of territory for settlement. Blackfeet are neither consulted, nor paid.

1874 Mounted Police detachment brings law and order to Canadian Blackfoot country and builds Fort Macleod.

Northern buffalo herd estimated at four million head, roaming Blackfoot country and centering around the Sweet Grass Hills.

1876 New Blackfoot Agency built on Badger Creek, within the new reduced reservation in Montana.

Blackfeet reject tobacco sent by Sioux, asking them to join in battle against whites, after Custer's defeat.

I.G. Baker of Fort Benton ships 75,000 buffalo robes to the East.

Ranchers and settlers begin to arrive in Canadian Blackfoot territory.

1877 Treaty Seven is signed at Blackfoot Crossing, in Canada. Siksika, Bloods and North Piegans permanently separate from South Piegans and the U.S. Government, although members from all the divisions continue to go back and forth across the border for some years, to collect treaty goods and payments.

Siksika chief Crowfoot becomes temporary "Chief of Blackfoot Confederacy."

1879 Buffalo virtually disappear from Canadian prairies, forcing government to issue beef rations to Canadian Blackfeet for first time.

South Piegans make last great Buffalo hunt in Judith Basin country of Montana.

1881 Mange epidemic said to have killed about half of Piegan horses, making younger warriors more eager to raid enemy camps, in spite of peace treaties signed by the older chiefs.

Winter Buffalo hunt in Montana not very successful.

1882 Large buffalo herd discovered on reservation, south of Sweet Grass Hills, though nothing like a few years before. Blackfeet make final tribal hunt. Each year, more Indians depend on government agency for food, as buffalo disappear.

1883 Only a few buffalo killed. About 3,000 Indians living by agency when rations start to run out, in late winter. Government red tape holds up additional food; people start starving. Agency gardens a complete failure, besides.

Blood Reserve is surveyed; head chief Red Crow leads Bloods to settle along the Belly River, in Canada.

1884 Last wild buffalo killed by Blackfeet; four lone animals, found near Sweet Grass Hills. Buffalo are now gone.

"Starvation Winter" kills several hundred South Piegans — from one-fourth to one-sixth of tribe — before sufficient rations arrive. Canadian Blackfeet fare somewhat better. About 2,000 surviving South Piegans settle within fifteen miles of their agency.

1889 Last Blackfoot war party to take enemy scalps leaves from Blood camps with combined group of Bloods and Piegans. So-called "Old Days" are now over.

1890 Learning a New Way of Life.

Blackfoot history begins its modern era, with each of the four divisions developing its own destiny, while the people maintain the overall spirit of the Blackfoot Confederacy.

As we near 100 years of this new way of living, members of the Blackfoot Confederacy will reflect with amazement at the tremendous changes in so short a time. Warriors and Buffalo women represented the Blackfoot Confederacy only 100 years ago!

Siksika warriors on the Alberta prairie, c. 1890.
(William Notman Photo)

14

White Calf, head chief of the South Piegans, or Montana Blackfeet; Old Agency, c. 1885.

(Smithsonian Institute Photo)

South Piegan Head Chiefs

NAME	BAND	TIME
"Sakatow" (Social chief)		1787
Kutenai Man (War chief)		1787
Lone Walker	Small Robes	1815
Big Lake		1846
Lame Bull (Lone chief)	Hard-Top-Knots	1855
Little Dog	Black-Patched-Moccasins	1866
Many Horses		1866
Big Lake	Hard-Top-Knots	1866
Little Plume	Worms	1876
Three Suns (Big Nose)	Fat Roasters	1877–1896
White Calf	Skunks	1877–1903

Upon the death of White Calf, in 1903, the office of head chief officially ended among the U.S. Blackfeet. By then, government agents gave all important orders on the reservation. Nevertheless, the people recognized certain individuals as symbolic of traditional chiefs and head chiefs.

The man to follow White Calf in this way was **Curly Bear,** starting in 1903. **Mountain Chief,** or Big Brave, was recognized by many, as was **Theodore Last Star.** Most recently the title of "honourary chief" was bestowed on long-time Blackfeet elected-leader **Earl Old Person.**

BELOW: Theodore Last Star on horseback, during a Pikunni - Blackfeet encampment; Browning, Montana, c. 1950.

(D.J. Schmidt Photo - Glacier Studio)

ABOVE: Five important men on the Blood Reserve in 1886. Left to right: One Spot, a minor chief; Red Crow, the head chief; Dave Mills, official interpreter; E.R. Cowan, missionary; W.B. Pocklington, government agent.

Blood Bands and Some of Their Chiefs

Lone Fighters: Jointly led by One Spot (who was also the assistant of head chief Red Crow) and Heavy Shield; later solely by Running Wolf.

Fish Eaters: The band of the head chiefs Bull's Back Fat, Seen-From-Afar, Red Crow and Crop-Eared-Wolf.

Bite Throats: Led by Low Horn.

Followers of the Buffalo: Led by Bull Horn. Earlier chief Bad Head, or Father-of-Many-Children.

Black Elks: Bull Shield, Eagle Head, and Blackfoot-Old-Woman.

Many Children: Young Pine. Earlier, Not-Scared-of-Gros Ventres.

Skinny People: Running Antelope.

Many Tumours: Strangling Wolf.

Bad People: Eagle Ribs.

Short People: Bull Back Fat.

BLOOD HEAD CHIEFS

South End Bloods			North End Bloods	
Bull Back Fat	c.	1820 - 1842	Rainy Chief	1860's- 1878
Bull Back Fat		1842 - 1850's	Running Rabbit	1878 - 1882
(close relative of above man)			Calf Tail	1883
Seen-From-Afar		1850's - 1869	Day Chief	1889 - 1907
Black Bear (elder bro. of above)		1869 - 1870	Blackfoot Old Woman	1907 - 1915
Red Crow (son of above)		1870 - 1900		
Crop Eared Wolf				
(adopted son of above)		1900 - 1913		

Combined Bloods after 1915

Shot-on-Both-Sides	1913 - 1958
Jim Shot-on-Both-Sides	1958 - 1964
Rufus Goodstriker	1964 - 1966
Jim Shot- n-Both-Sides	1966 - 1980
Roy Fox	1980 -

Blood Reserve Facts in 1888

2,135 people, divided into 21 bands, led by one head chief and 18 minor chiefs. That year, there were born 51 boys and 34 girls, died 41 boys and 23 girls, along with 51 adults.

Daily ration amounted to 1.09 pounds of beef and .37 pounds of flour. There were 216 houses, 51 built during that year. There were 240 broke acres, 335 fenced; 986 bushels of potatoes were grown on 33 acres, with more lost to dry rot. Also grown were 1,356 bushels of oats, on 90 acres, 56 bushels of wheat on 3 acres, and 25 acres of mixed vegetables.

ABOVE: Yellow Horn, Peigan head chief, 1936.

NORTH PEIGAN HEAD CHIEFS

1877 - 1886	Eagle Tail
1886 - 1890	North Axe
1891 - 1901	Crow Eagle
1902 - 1921	Black Plume
	(Leaning Over Butchering)
1922 - 1929	Philip Big Swan
1933 - 1949	Yellow Horn
1951 - 1962	John Yellow Horn
1963 - 1964	Peter Smith
1965 - 1976	Maurice McDougall
1977 - 1982	Nelson Small Legs
1983 - 1988	Peter Yellowhorn
1989 -	Leonard Bastien

Treaty 7 Chiefs: Eagle Tail
                           Morning Plume
                           Big Swan
                           Crow Eagle

Crow Eagle, Peigan head chief, 1900. (Edward S. Curtis Photo)

ABOVE: Siksika leaders inside the tribal Medicine Lodge of 1921. Head chief Yellow Horse is in the black hat and striped blanket, leaning against the sacred Center Pole. Only Chief is the old man in the foreground, a tribal leader. Three Suns is wearing a white scarf and light hat; he was a renowned warrior, rich and popular in his old age.
(H. Pollard Collection - Provincial Museum and Archives of Alberta)

ABOVE: Chiefs of the Blackfoot Confederacy, visiting Ottawa, c. 1890. Left to right: North Axe, head chief of the North Peigans; Three Bulls, brother-in-law and advisor to Crowfoot; Siksika head chief Crowfoot, the only man ever considered head chief of all the Blackfoot Confederacy, at the time of signing Treaty No. Seven, 13 years before this photo; Red Crow, head chief of the Bloods; One Spot, minor chief and advisor to Red Crow.

(Public Archives Canada - PA 66624)

HEAD CHIEFS OF THE SIKSIKA
(with approximate years in office)

Crowfoot	c. 1870 - 1899	Joseph Crowfoot	1950 - 1958
Old Sun	c. 1900 - 1905	Clarence McHugh	1958 - 1964
(leader of west side people)		Joseph Crowfoot	1964 - 1968
Iron Shield	c. 1900 - 1912	Percy Yellow Fly	1968 - 1972
(leader of east side people)		Leo Pretty Young Man	1972 - 1980
Running Rabbit	c. 1905 - 1912	Roy Little Chief	1980 - 1982
(replaced Old Sun)		Strater Crowfoot	1988 -
Yellow Horse	1912 - 1920's		
Duck Chief	1920's - 1950		
(son of Running Rabbit)			

Blackfoot Geography in Montana

Armell Creek: *Itiskiotsope*, or "it-crushed-them," referring to a cutbank along this creek which collapsed and buried a number of people digging for sacred paint.

Augusta: *Spitzee*, or "tall trees."

Bear Paw Mountains: *Kiyayo-otsii-stukists*, or "Bear Hand Mountains."

Bear Tooth Mountains: *Makwi-ochpeekin*, or "Wolf Tooth."

Belt Mountains: *Maipsi-istuk*, "belt mountain," referring to a rim of rock that encircles a butte in this range.

Bighorn Mountains: *Meeki-istukists*, or "red mountains."

Bighorn River: *Omachkskinnae-sisachta*, "bighorn river."

Buffalo Lake: *Omachk-iniskim*, or "big buffalo stone." An Iniskim is a stone of peculiar shape, sometimes found near this lake, which becomes a good-luck charm once it has been blessed and properly handled by one skilled in its ceremony. Most Blackfoot families had such stones.

Choteau: *Nissoe-tuppi*, "four persons," referring to four Crow warriors killed here during a battle between their tribe and the Pikunni. A place nine miles north of town is noted as *Akoch-soatsis-otsitotope*, or "Many-Tail-Feathers burned it," referring to the last active buffalo pound used by the Pikunni and burnt by a man of that name after he was instructed to do so in a dream, because too many buffalo were being wasted.

Conrad: *Akai-ochkotokskui-ksiskum*, or "Many Rocks Spring," referring to a spring about ten miles east of town, where Pikunni war parties often came in winter for the fresh, open water.

Cutbank Creek: *Inobissie*, or "hung themselves down," referring to a place at the head of this creek where a Gros Ventre war party lowered themselves over a cliff with ropes in order to surprise a war party of Pikunni.

Cutbank River: *Piksikseen-aksiskum*, or "snake spring."

Dearborn River: *Awotahn-otsitamistsi*, or "where the shield floated down," referring to the time a shield fell from a pack horse and floated off down the river.

East Butte: *Imoyistsimokan*, or "Hairy Cap."

Fort Benton: *Akahpioyis*, or "Many Houses."

Fort Conrad: *Sisuckikayi-istsimokan*, or "Spotted Cap," that being the Indian name of Charles Conrad, one of the fort's founders.

Great Falls: *Ibumi-stuckskui*, or "Rock Ridge Across."

Heart Butte: *Uskitsipchpi-istuki*, or "Heart Butte."

Helena: *Ochkotokoatsis-ksachkum*, or "Many Sharp Points Land," referring to the numerous cacti growing here.

Judith Gap: *Itsipohtsi-stuckuyi*, or "Mountains coming from Both Sides."

Judith Mountains: *Otachkui-istaki*, or "Yellow Mountains."

Judith River: *Otachkui-itachta*, or "Yellow River," at the mouth of which was signed the "Lame Bull Treaty"of 1855.

Lame Deer: *Omachk-itumoi*, or "Big Butte."

Little Rocky Mountains: *Makwi-istakists*, or "Wolf Mountains."

Marias River: *Kiyaiyo-isisachta*, or "Bear River."

Milk River: *Kinuk-sisachta*, or "Little River."

Musselshell River: *Kiyaiyo-isisachta*, or "Bear River," though the upper part was better known as *Otsistsi-itachta*, or "Shell River." This was the southern boundary of Blackfoot country according to the 1855 Treaty.

Pryor Creek: *Apsi-itachta*, or "Arrow Creek," so called because men on the war trail used to shoot arrows for good luck up into an inaccessible cave near the top of a cutbank along this creek.

Pryor Mountains: *Auwachpitsi-istukiks*, or "Lonesome Mountains," because they seem so rough, barren and unfriendly.

Red River: *Amochk-itachta*, or "Red River."

St. Mary Lake: *Pachtomachski-kimeeks*, or "Lakes Inside," because the two lakes by this name (upper and lower) are surrounded by mountains.

Shelby: *Nitsisahn-kauwachko*, or "Paint Coulee."

Silver City: *Sisikskim-itachtai*, or "Black Metal Creek."

Sweetgrass Hills: *Kutoyisiks*, or "Sweet Pines," a different kind of incense than Sweetgrass.

Teton River: *Munikees-sisokchta*, or "Breast River."

Timber Creek: *Maisto-omachksim-otsitauwatsapps*, or "Where Big Raven Went Crazy." Big Raven was said to have been a Pikunni chief who one day took off his clothes to swim in this river, coming out of the water singing and refusing to ever put his clothes on again.

Two Medicine Lake: *Natoki-okoyists-omachksikimi*, or "Two Medicine Lodges Lake," recalling a time of urgent need among the Pikunni during which two Sun Lodges were put up at the same time, here.

Wolf Creek: *Atsinai-itomohtsah*, or "Where Gros Ventres were massacred," recalling a victorious battle for the Pikunni.

Yellowstone Park: *Akai-seetsi*, or "Many Smokes," referring to the geysers and hot springs.

Yellowstone River: *Ponokai-sisokchta*, or "Elk River."

Pikunni - Blackfeet in Glacier National Park (Glacier Studio)

24

Blackfoot Geography in Alberta

Arrowwood: *Mists-akaitapisko*, or "wood village."

Banff: *Nato-siskum*, or "holy springs." The hot springs were visited by passing Blackfeet for their medicinal value.

Bassano: *Pusahnai*, being the closest that Blackfoot could come to pronouncing this town's European name.

Beaver Mines: *Estai-sachta*, "where we get paint." Named for a small deposit of dark ceremonial paint found near here.

Blairmore: *Nitaistato-ksistokyopi*, or "where they tear logs," named for one of the region's first sawmills, built there in the 1890's.

Brocket: *Pikunniowa-otsitonipi*, or "where the Piegans have their father," meaning Piegan Agency.

Brooks: *Pik-sik-see*, or "Snake," the Blackfoot name for the first storekeeper in this area.

Calgary: *Moch-ghinstsis*, or "elbow," because of the large bend of the Bow River, here.

Cardston: *Ahgochkimi*, or "many wives;" early Mormon settlers shared the Blackfoot custom of one man having several wives.

Claresholm: *Asoyee-napi-oyis*, or "barrel-whiteman-house," after the small settlement got its own water tower. This name was used for other similar places, as well.

Cluny: *Siksistoyi*, "Black Mustache," the Indian name of a local storekeeper.

Coaldale: *Inuk-akaitapisko*, "little place where we buy," or "small town," a common name.

Coleman: *Asakots-akaitapisko*, "beer town," a place where illegal liquor was available.

Coutts: *Isksaksin*, "the line," referring to the International Boundary.

Cowley: *Akai-saukas*, "many prairie turnips," a popular place to dig these edible roots.

Crowsnest: *Maisto-ghoa*, "Crow's nest," referring to a war party of Crow Indians who made a legendary last stand in the heights of Crowsnest Mountain.

Del Bonita: *Kai-kimikai*, "opening through the ridge."

Drumheller: *Pistan-akaitapisko*, "coulee town."

Edmonton: *Omach-kuyis*, "big house," because of a three-storey loghouse built within Fort Edmonton in 1831.

Etzikom: *Istsikoom*, "coulee."

Fort Macleod: *Akapiyoyis*, or "many houses," because it was the region's first large settlement with buildings. Noted among these was the *Inukapiyoyis*, or "seizer's house," seizers being the mounted policemen. An ancient name for this part of the Oldman River is *Itoy-aistoyi-okoa*, or "where they painted the Crow lodge," referring to the Crow-painted tipi, which was first dreamed here. It is still in use among the Blackfeet.

Frank: *Awawakai*, or "slide," referring to the disastrous rock slide in 1903. An ancient name was "holy springs," for the sulphur waters nearby.

Gleichen: *Sokitsi*, or "fat stomach," in honour of that town's first storekeeper.

Glenwood: *Mists-akaitapisko*, or "wood village," common name for places near river bottoms.

High River: *Spitzee*, or "tall trees." Also called "north tall trees," by the North Piegans, who call Pincher Creek "Spitzee."

Hillspring: *Muksiskom-akaitapisko*, or "spring town."

Lethbridge: *Sikoch-otok*, or "black rock," for the coal deposits. Also called *Aksaisim*, or "steep banks."

Magrath: *Ksamuskini*, or "hump back," for the first storekeeper.

Medicine Hat: *Sah-ahms*, or "sacred headdress," in reference to a legendary encounter with the Crees in which the Blackfeet obtained a special headdress.

Monarch: *Iyakskik-sakukoi*, or "left-hand bend" of the Oldman River.

Namaka: *Inuksikoki*, or "little corner." Namaka comes from the Blackfoot word *Namachtai*, referring to the Bow River, but that was not its Indian name.

Okotoks: *Ochkotoksitachtai*, or "stone river." Okotoks comes from the Blackfoot word *ochkodoks*, referring to unusual glacial boulders in the area.

Pekisko: *Pikisko*, or "rough ridge."

Picture Butte: *Anatskim-ikui*, or "pretty hill."

Pincher Creek: *Spitzee*, or "tall trees." Called by the Siksika "south tall trees," to tell it from High River, which has the same name.

Ponoka: *Awatsapsi-okoa*, or "crazy house," because of the mental hospital there. *Ponoka* is the Blackfoot word for elk, many of which used to roam on the prairies.

Raymond: *Itiya-pinokaup*, or "where we make sugar," referring to the sugar refinery where many Blackfeet have worked.

Red Deer: *Ponoka-sisachta*, or "elk river;" the red deer being a European's reaction to elk.

Rocky Mountain House: *Kitsapuyoysis*, or "above house," to tell it from the main "house," or trading post, downriver at Fort Edmonton.

Spring Coulee: *Okayaksin*, or "dammed place," for St. Mary Dam.

Standoff: *Itatouktai* or "where the rivers meet," referring to the Belly and Waterton Rivers. Nearby Belly Buttes are called *Mokoans*. More recent name for Standoff is *Sapoyi*, or "standing apart."

Stirling: *Omachkotsi-mokoi*, or "big meadow grass."

Strathmore: *Omachksikoki*, or "big corner," referring to a bend in the trail to the Calgary area.

Taber: *Itasoyope*, or "where we eat from," meaning literally, "table." This is from a misunderstanding by Indians who first heard the name Taber.

Twin Butte: *Natsikapaitomo*, or "double hill."

Vulcan: *Motoksin-akaitapisko*, or "knee town," referring to nearby hills in the shape of a knee.

Waterton: *Pachtomachksi-kimee*, or "inside lake," because it is within the Rocky Mountains.

Wetaskiwin: *Inustsitomo*, or "peace hills," referring to nearby hills where peace was once made between Blackfeet and Cree.

Whoop-Up: *Akai-nuskwi*, or "many dead," recalling a smallpox epidemic that once struck a camp here.

The Okan

Origin Story of the Blackfoot "Sun Dance," or Medicine Lodge Ceremony
Told by Ben Calf Robe in 1977

This is actually a very long story, how it all happened. Here I am just telling the main parts of it. I have sponsored Medicine Lodges among my Siksika people, so I am qualified to talk about it. I want to encourage the younger generations to carry on with these things our ancestors learned long ago.

On a particular day in that long-ago time, before our people had horses, or celebrated the Okan, some girls were out by their tipis, looking up at the sky. It was evening time, but it was just like daylight. The moon was full and out, and all the Stars were shining. One pretty young girl suddenly said: "Ki-eye-yah!"(A Blackfoot woman's expression)."That one Star that is shining so bright, that is the one that I will marry!" Everyone heard her say it, but they didn't say anything back. Soon they all went home to bed.

The next day was coming to evening when the same girl went out to gather Buffalo chips. In those days the women would go out every evening for a supply of chips to put on their fires. They would stay warm all night and in the morning they would still be glowing. The girl was out with her mother.

On their way back home the girl had to fix her broken carrying strap. Her mother said, "Hurry up; it is dark already." The girl told her to just go ahead, because she couldn't make it fast enough. Then she saw a pair of feet right in front of her. She looked up and saw a very handsome young man. She asked him, "Why is it you are here?" He told her he was the Star she said she would marry. Then he told her to put down her load of chips and to stand on a calf hide with him, but to close her eyes. When he told her to open them again, she was high in the sky.

The man told her: "The women come here to dig turnips, and you can join them; but don't ever dig up that Big Turnip, because we only eat the small ones." And so she lived in the Sky . . . .

Everything went well for some time. She used to go with the other women to dig turnips. Then one day she thought she would just dig up that Big Turnip to see how large it was. She worked hard with her stick, and dug all around it, until it was loose. Then she took hold of it good and she pulled it out. There was a big hole in the ground and when she looked into it she could look through the Sky and down to the Earth, below. She saw the camps of her people, and she started to cry.

Her husband figured out that she had dug up the Big Turnip. He told her: "All right, you have dug it up; so I will have to let you go back home. But you will take some things back with you to help your people, to bring them together."

That is when she was first shown about the Sun Dance, the Okan. Because she was a virtuous girl, she was given these things to bring to the people. She was taught about the forked Centre Pole—its meaning as the center of the Universe—also about the posts that go around it and the rawhide that ties them all together. She was taught the songs for it, and what it all means. She was shown the different incense altars, and the use of Earth paints that go with the Okan. This was a miracle! A big mystery, how she learned it all, because it is very long and complicated. Finally she was ready to be lowered back down to Earth, at the end of a magic rawhide.

Back in the camp it was afternoon, and a lot of the people were sitting outside, visiting and playing. There was a boy lying on his back, looking up at the sky. Suddenly he told his mother, "Na-ah" (an intimate word for mother, and grandmother), "there is something strange coming down from the Sky." His mother was very involved in a game, so she just told him, "Oh, you must have some goops in your eyes!" But as the girl got near the ground others saw her too. Finally she got down, and she went right to her parents' tipi. Pretty soon all the old wise people were called to come and hear what the girl had to say, and she told them about the Okan. She sang the songs and explained the different things that she had been taught.

The people all saw her coming down from the Sky, so they believed her story the way she told it. The wise elders councilled and decided to go ahead with a Sun Dance right away. There was one man that time who had the Beaver Bundle, and he was very smart, so he was put in charge of the Okan ceremony.

There is a long story about how the Elk rubbed his horns on the Centre Pole to knock off the Holy Woman's sacred headdress, the one we call the Natoas. He didn't manage to knock it down, because the Elk-woman won with her "power," instead, and she said it should be used as the sacred headdress from then on. This headdress used to be kept by the Beaver Man, in his Beaver Bundle. He learned the special Natoas songs, to go along with all the other songs he knew, which were for nearly every bird and animal.

The Holy Woman was taught to carry a hide and a digging stick, just like the girl who went up to the Sky and learned about the Okan in the first place. It all originated from that time, and then other things were added with the passing of time to make the Sun Dance larger.

It eventually came to be that everything had a part in the Okan, or Sun Dance. All the different societies came into the Okan lodge to sing, dance and confess their war deeds. The Weather Dancers were there to pray, dance and keep good weather. The Beaver Men were the leaders, because the songs for the Sun Dance are like the ones for the Beaver Bundles. The Medicine Pipes go in there to be smoked; that is the only time they can be smoked among us Blackfeet. It is very mysterious how all these holy things were made to go together for the Sun Dance, and today we are still seeing it carried on.

BELOW: The last Medicine Lodge, or Okan, built at Two Medicine Lake in Glacier National Park, 1915.   (Thomas B. Magee Photo)

28

How They Made the Sun Dance Camp in my Youth

Told by Ben Calf Robe

I remember well the Sun Dance camps from my boyhood. That was the biggest event in our tribal life in those days. Everybody came to them and took part—men and women, young and old. There must have been hundreds of camps in a very big circle. My parents were always very active in what went on, so I grew up knowing about it.

The people move to the Sun Dance grounds after the Motokiks have had their four days of ceremonies. The Medicine Pipe Owners are the first ones to break their camp and move. All the People will watch them to see which way to go. That is why the Medicine Pipes have always been owned by chiefs. The People will follow along behind, while the Medicine Pipe Owners and their wives go ahead with the Pipe Bundles.

During this move to the Sun Dance the Bumblebees have their dance. They are the youngest society group in the All Friends Association. They are just little boys who are learning about life. They attack the People who are moving camp, just like a swarm of bees. They have Eagle claws and they use them to scratch the People who are not moving fast enough. The older societies have their dances after the camp gets set up.

The Medicine Pipe Owners sing and pray as they lead the way, and other People pray, also. There were no cars or other distractions. Everyone was quiet and the camps were kept neat. The Medicine Pipe Owners have their tipis a little ways into the centre of the camp circle. The rest of the People put their camps in a line further out, so they will notice where the Medicine Pipes are. The only other tipis that go in towards the centre are for the Horns Society and for women who are going to put up the Okan.

As soon as the camps get set up the husband of the one that is putting up the Sun Dance has to take a sweat bath. They call one of the middle-aged societies—the Pigeons or the Crazy Dogs—to go and get the willows and rocks to prepare the sweathouse. They have to get 100 willow sticks and 100 rocks. The Sweathouse and the rocks will be painted, one half black and the other red. The man will go inside and sweat with the one who is giving him the initiation, and other holy men. The Holy Woman and the helpers sit outside the sweatlodge and pray. After that they have to stay secluded in the Holy Woman's tipi and sing songs for four days.

After the camp is set up and the sacred sweat is over, the Horns Society begins to meet and have ceremonies. They are the eldest among the societies. In my dad's time there was a Bulls Society that was for really old men, but it died out long before me. These Horns are also very powerful and secret. They sing and pray and have dances for four days and nights, like the Motokiks. They have a lot of their ceremonies inside, so you can only hear them. But they come out to dance around the camps in the daytime, and that is when they show off their sacred Staffs and Headdresses that belong inside their Medicine Bundles. I belonged to this society for nineteen years and I went through all of the secret initiations, some of them more than once.

During these first four days all kinds of holy events take place, one after another. The ones that are going to transfer Medicine Pipes announce the day of their ceremony to the camp. They transfer Medicine tipis and shields, headdresses and Weasel suits, and all kinds of charms and necklaces. Back then there were lots of Horses. Everyone brought their herd along to the camps and they used them to make transfer payments, along with blankets and other valuables.

During these four days, when holy things are going on all over, the announcer goes around the camp all the time to tell the People what is taking place. Finally, he tells them to go out and cut the posts. Each band is told to cut two forked posts and two straight poles, one much longer than the other. These will make the frame of the Medicine Lodge. Some of the members ride out for these, while others dig the post holes according to the directions of older men.

Sometimes I was the one who dug the big hole for the Center Pole. My mother encouraged me in this, saying: "Whoever digs this main hole lives a long life, so you always dig it when you can." It was hard work, deep down. When I finish digging my mother always comes over and she gives me some tobacco and she prays while I put it in the bottom of the hole, as an offering.

Now, the four days go by quickly and then comes the big part of the celebration. They put up a canvas Sun-shelter near the Medicine Lodge for the Holy People who are putting up the Sun Dance (or Medicine Lodge, both have the same meaning in tradition). Practically all the Sun Dance ceremony has been transferred to the Holy Woman and her husband by this time. Only the raising of the Center Pole has to be initiated, then they will be through with their part of the Sun Dance.

The Holy Woman is led outside and she stands on a robe, facing the Sun. They open one of the parfleches filled with the blessed tongues. These are the Sacraments. One of the Motoki women takes a piece of tongue and hands it to the Holy Woman. She raises it towards the Sun and she prays hard. She makes her confessions in front of all the People, so they will know if she ever came close to losing her virtuousness. Then she starts breaking off pieces of the tongue and the People all come forward to "Eat Holy with the Sun." All the parfleches are full of tongues, so they have enough for everybody in the camp.

When they are finished giving out the Sacrament someone brings in a fresh hide. Some of the very old People are brought up to call their most famous war coups before the hide can be cut. It is the same as with the Holy Woman; they are confessing their hardest deeds before the Sun and the People. The hide is cut into strips that are used to tie up the Medicine Lodge poles.

The Motokiks ride out with members of one of the younger societies to get branches that are tied in a big bunch into the fork of the Centre Pole. The Horns are the ones that cut the Centre Pole and bring it in. An old warrior tells coups for the cutting. The society women wear wreaths of leaves around their heads for this work, which is holy. They are all singing and praying as they go along.

While they are gone for the Centre Pole and branches, the Holy People sit inside of the Sun-shelter that was put up by the Medicine Lodge. The People line up outside and bring Offerings. These are made with sticks in the shape of a cross, to which are tied bunches of Sage, Eagle feathers, and a hide or piece of cloth. The Holy People bless each family that brings an offering, and smokes their pipe that they come prepared with. The Offerings get tied to the Medicine Lodge to take the prayers to the Above Spirits.

Sometimes the Medicine Pipe Owners bring out their Holy Pipes, along with an Offering. This is very special, because it is the only time that the Medicine Pipe Stem is ever smoked. The People move back and let the Medicine Pipes through to the Holy People inside the shelter. Even Beaver Bundle Pipes were brought out and smoked at this time.

30

When the Centre Pole is in place, lying by the hole it goes in, the Holy People go around it and the husband of the Holy Woman climbs up on the end of it with the man who is initiating him. They will pray and sing a certain song, during which the Centre Pole is given a shaking to ensure it will stand up good. The Holy Woman's husband spreads out his robe and it is painted black. At the same time they make marks on the Pole for how many days the Weather Dancers will keep the Sun Dance going after this. Sometimes it was four days, other times just two.

At this point the whole camp is ready to help "put up the Medicine Lodge." All around the camp circle they are standing in pairs, carrying tipi poles that are tied together at the tips, two at a time. They stand like that and sing, outside their lodges. The whole camp is singing, and they move towards the Centre slowly. They stop four times, then they all shout and hook their tied poles at different places on the Centre Pole. Some have ropes that they tie to the top and then they start pulling and pushing to raise the Centre Pole. All this time there is lots of shouting and shooting. A lot of the men have guns and some of the boys have bows with blunt arrows, and they shoot into the fork of the Centre Pole, as it slips gently into the hole. The Offerings made by the People in the camp have already been tied to the tips of the long poles. They push these up into the fork of the Centre Pole and then they use the strips of freshly cut hide to tie down the butt ends. It all happens very quickly and the Lodge is finished. The Holy Woman is finished with her duties. Her husband jumps off the Pole just as it gets raised. To finish his duties he takes another sweat bath.

The Holy People leave a buffalo skull at the base of the Centre Pole. They made it holy during a ceremony in which they paint it, half red and half black, and they stuff the openings with Sage. When the Medicine Lodge is built the People all go back to their own homes, including the Holy Woman and her husband. Then the announcer goes around the camp to give the next instructions.

"Hurry up and get your Horses and ride for the brush to cover the Holy Lodge," he will say. Boys and girls and men and women all join in to go — whoever wants to. That time there were no cars, so they all rode on Horses. They decorate their Horses with beadwork and bells, and they all dress up fancy, just like a parade. They run out to the bushes on their horses and they cut lots of long branches. They all bring ropes that they tie to their branches, so they can pull them along behind. Then they all ride back into camp in a long, wide row. They all sing the old Sun Dance song, everybody knows it. That is a very powerful time. They ride into the center of the camp and they drop off their loads by the Medicine Lodge so that they cover up the sides of it. They just leave an opening to the East, for a doorway. When the Lodge is covered, thick and green, then they stop for the night.

The next morning the Weather Dancers take over. That is the only important thing that I was never initiated to, so I cannot say too much about it. They dress up in their special ways and they have certain ceremonies to help the People and to keep the weather good. People come to them to be painted and blessed, and incense is made by them. They sit in a special booth at the back of the Medicine Lodge. The Holy People sit on one side of them and the Sun Dance drummers sit on the other side. That is when they have the Digging Dance.

In those days there were many different societies, so they announced in the camp which society would start in the Medicine Lodge with the digging dance. Members of all the societies got dressed up in their best — they brought whatever was transferred to them or used in war. Their women made Berry Soups and other food, and they start singing. They come to the Medicine Lodge in groups, singing. The Motokiks sit on

31

ABOVE: A scene inside one of the last Medicine Lodges put up by the Siksika, around 1960. Four days and nights of fasting and ceremonial work led to the construction of this brush-covered lodge, which symbolizes a sacred home for the Sun and all Creation, including the people. Society dances and other ceremonies take place inside this lodge, including the ritual of piercing those who have made vows during times of need. This piercing was outlawed in the 1890's; the scene in this photo is only a re-enactment, though the practice has recently been revived. The dancer is Jack Kipp; advisors include One Gun, on the right, Turned-Up Nose, on the left, and Ben Calf Robe in blanket and headdress.

(Glenbow - Alberta Institute Photo)

one side, inside the Medicine Lodge, and the Horns sit on the other, and everyone sings. It is a very spiritual thing to watch. Every once in a while they get up to dance. They dance in two lines, one on each side, back and forth. They bring their rifles and they do a lot of shooting and shouting.

After a while they serve out the food that they brought — big piles of it. When everyone is finished eating they call some old person forward who has a lot of brave deeds to his record. They have already initiated someone to dig a big hole in front of the Centre Pole. This old man will count his *coups* with the sticks, then use them to start the fire. When he is finished his enemy-friend (a life-long joking rival) will get up and say, "No, he is not brave; those are nothing, that he did; what I've done is much better; and so on." Then he will count his *coups* and throw sticks into the fire for them. And they go on like that, sometimes for a couple of days.

When I was young there were still a lot of men with big war stories. Even the young men were still going out to raid Horses from ranchers and other tribes, although the fighting was over.

During the days that the Weather Dancers are in charge all the different societies come into the Medicine Lodge to sing their songs and dance. The Weather Dancers have a lot of songs of their own, too. And a lot of old People and relatives of the society members sing praise songs for the ones they want to honor. It is a time of great celebration for the People.

Yellow Horse was a head chief after the time of Crowfoot. His wife was my grandmother, in the Indian way. She was a Holy Woman. That is, she put up lots of Sun Dances, because she was always true to her husband. She was the Holy Woman for my first Sun Dance. Here is how it happened:

It was around the year 1929. I had my first boy that time. He was outside playing in the corral. Nobody saw him go out there. He crawled under one of my Horses and it kicked him. My sister was working in the house, by the window, and she saw him get kicked. She ran out and found my little boy with a big gash on his forehead. He looked pretty bad, so she made the vow right there — she called out to the Sun to save my boy, and she promised to help that old lady, Natoki-sisoyah, to make the Sun Dance. We got the boy to the hospital and after he recovered he was all right.

I didn't take an active part in that first ceremony. I was just painted and initiated, but the older People did all the ceremonial work. I paid for most of the ceremony. I gave up all my best Horses, including my three favorite work Horses that I bought from a white rancher. They made a big corral outside the Holy Lodge where the Horses were kept for everyone to see. My sister contributed about ten or fifteen herd Horses, but I gave a lot more. I even paid for the sacred sweatbath, where they gave the Sacrament. It is our custom to pay for every part of a holy initiation. The more sacrifices you make, the more valuable your initiation will be in the future. This is how we show our appreciation to the person who is giving up his holy rights and powers for you. I provided enough Hudson Bay blankets, and other dry goods, to cover the whole path where the Holy Woman and her attendants walked to give out the sacred-tongue-sacrament. Mrs. Big Snake was the one who got all these things. Her relatives came and gathered them up.

ABOVE:For each Blackfoot Sun Dance there are one or two Weather Dancers, who sit in a special place of honour on the west side of the brush-covered Medicine Lodge. Their dress and other symbols are part of initiated mysteries that help them in maintaining good weather. This scene was taken around 1900, at the time of Ben Calf Robe's youth. It shows his uncle Calf Bull, on the right, with Black Bull, who was also called Yellow Old Woman.
(Pollard Photo, Provincial Museum and Archives of Alberta)

ABOVE: Deer painted lodge and Crow painted lodge; in a Pikunni - Blackfeet Sun Dance camp, c. 1950. (D.J. Schmidt Photo - Glacier Studio)

Painted Lodges

It has always been easy to recognize Blackfoot camps because of their distinctive painted lodges. Only certain tipis were decorated, since ceremonies had to be performed before families could use designs on them. Each painted lodge represents the mystical experiences of some wise Blackfoot. In today's tipi camps, these lodges are like pages from a book of Blackfoot spiritual history.

For instance, one man of long, long ago (Blackfoot history does not consist of written dates) lived a life of misfortune, until one day his Spirit wandered away and learned about a new tipi design. It did this by going underwater, in a big lake, where it found a beautiful lodge that was the home of an old, grey-haired Otter. This Otter spoke, sang songs, and moved around like a person. It taught that man's Spirit what became known as the "Otter Lodge ceremony," which is still carried on today.

That man's body was unconscious, or maybe asleep, while all this was happening to his Spirit. When it returned to him, he awoke, and his mind recalled everything his Spirit had seen. It made him very happy to know about the Otter's ceremony; he felt very good about it. Back at his camp, he got advice from leading elders, who helped him paint his own lodge like the one his Spirit had seen. They also helped him sing the Otter's songs and to perform its ceremonies. After that his luck changed, and he continued feeling good about life. He became a noted man within the Blackfoot Confederacy, and his lodge design was highly regarded.

Eventually others who had had bad luck thought things might get better if *they* had this man's Otter Lodge, and the rights to its ceremony. They had faith in its ability to improve their life, so they asked the man to transfer it. He agreed, and the ceremony was performed. Sure enough, misfortune changed to good luck for the new owners. Thus, respect for the original owner's spiritual experience—and for the lodge design which symbolized it—grew even more among the Blackfoot people. To show their appreciation, the new owners shared the best of their success with the original man, in the form of food, clothing, and war trophies. That was their sacrifice for the blessings they had been given. It was a form of making payment.

Stories similar to this go along with every Blackfoot tipi design (and with every medicine bundle), although in recent years some of the lodge origins and ceremonies have been lost and forgotten. A number of the designs, themselves, have disappeared from the camp circles after their last owners died without passing on the transfer ceremonies. In other cases, tipi designs have been copied by persons (both Indian and white) unable or unwilling to go through the proper ceremonies. Of course, this is contrary to Blackfoot customs and ceremonial rules.

List of Painted Tipi Designs
Transferred among the Bloods

1906 List, compiled by Clark Wissler		*1966 List, from Joe Gambler*	
1. Big-Striped	14. Horse	1. Buffalo Head	12. Hoof (Buffalo)
2. Mountain Goat	15. Buffalo Hoof	2. Head Down	13. Fish
3. Wolverine	16. Yellow	3. Skunk	14. Snake
4. Bear	17. Otter	4. Half-Black	15. Striped
5. Fisher	18. Horse	5. Sheep	16. Rib
6. Elk	19. Snake	6. Prairie Chicken	17. All-Painted
7. Half-Black	20. Water-Monster	7. Horse	18. Half-Yellow
8. Bald Eagle	21. Buffalo Head	8. War	19. Half-Yellow Otter
9. All-Over	22. Skunk	9. War *(second type)*	20. Gnawed (Ice)
10. War	23. Fish	10. Otter	21. Downward Star
11. Crane	24. Space	11. Yellow	22. Across
12. All-Stars	25. Centre		
13. Prairie Chicken			

Blackfoot Tipi Etiquette

Some Blackfoot families still camp regularly in tipis, setting up more or less a traditional household, even if a modern car or truck waits nearby to drive them back into modern life, afterwards. For tribal encampments, spiritual ceremonies, or as a summer place next to one's regular house, tipi life can do much to recharge the energies of those who take part in it.

The center of tipi life is the fireplace. From the beginning, kids are taught to keep away from it. "Play with fire and you will be burned" was a common warning. For the same reason, kids were generally forbidden to get too "lively" inside a tipi, and guests were expected to sit down and stay in one place.

Upon entering a tipi, guests usually wait by the door until they've been shown where to sit. Honoured guests are always given comfortable places "at the back", opposite the door, usually next to the man and woman of the household (the head woman, where there was more than one wife). If they were young people, or just regular folks from the camp, their seat was closer to the door, leaving the back available for more important persons. In any case, women went to the left and men to the right, husbands and wives sitting down across from each other, with the fire in the middle.

Visitors in traditional Blackfoot lodges *never* walk in front of the host and his wife, nor between the fireplace and any other important guest. Ceremonial rules strictly forbid this, especially if the guest is smoking.

Visitors should not disturb the host of an important guest. If joining them, this should be done quietly, without attracting needless attention. A good visitor does not start out by doing a lot of talking, nor is one expected to ask a lot of questions.

BELOW: Inside a Piegan-Blackfeet tipi; Wades-in-the-Water and wife Julia, c. 1950.
(D.J. Schmidt Photo - Glacier Studio)

Blackfoot girl with her own painted tipi. Daughter of a band chief, honour and blessings were bestowed on her with the ceremonial transfer of the sacred tipi design. For this, her parents gave many horses and goods. (Edward S. Curtis Photo)

Contemporary Statistics
of the
Blackfoot Confederacy

Blackfoot Reserve: 50 kms. east of Calgary. 71,014 hect. (17,406 acres). 1983 Census: 3,182. 60% of reserve suitable for agriculture. Major crops include wheat and perennial forages. Main Communities: Gleichen and Cluney. Tribe has own schools, museum, medical facilities and police. Siksika Resort includes golf course, lake, camping, tennis, etc.

Blood Reserve: 15 kms. west of Lethbridge. 141,490 hect. (349,618 acres), plus timber reserve adjacent to Waterton National Park of 1,971 hect. (4,872 acres). 1981 Census: 6,149. Main communities: Stand Off, Cardston and Laverne. Economy includes cattle ranching, farming, oil and gas leases, Kainai Industries home building. Tribe has its own farm, schools, hospital, policing, administration complex, newspaper and radio production, plus numerous private businesses.

Peigan Reserve: (Note the name is spelled Peigan in Canada, Piegan in the U.S.):60 kms. west of Lethbridge. 45,609 hect. (112,656 acres), bisected by the Old Man River. 1984 Census: 1,945. Main community, Brocket. Band has timber reserve in Porcupine Hills. Economy includes cattle, farming, Peigan Ranches Ltd., Peigan Developments Ltd., Peigan Bus Co-Op, Pe-Kun-nee Garments, plus private gas station and other businesses. Band has its own schools and police.

Blackfeet Reservation: Northwestern Montana, adjacent to Glacier National Park. Total reservation land: 906,441 acres. 1969 Census: 10,467 enrolled, 6,220 resident. 1980: 5,525 resident. Main towns and communities: Browning, Babb, Heart Butte, Starr School, East Glacier. 90% of tribal income is from minerals, especially oil and gas. 10% from miscellaneous, including ranching, farming and timber. Tribe has schools, hospital, police and court system. Owns the Blackfeet Indian Writing Company, a modern pen and pencil factory. Many private businesses operated by tribe members.

Blackfoot Bibliography

There have been a great many books written about the Blackfoot Confederacy. Most of them are out of print and hard to find. The following list includes only those books that the authors have found of particular value, especially in compiling this book.

Calf Robe, Ben, with **Adolf & Beverly Hungry Wolf.** *Siksika, A Blackfoot Legacy,* Good Medicine Books, Invermere, 1979.

Ewers, John C. *The Blackfeet: Raiders on the Northwestern Plains,* University of Oklahoma Press, Norman, 1958.

— — —. *The Horse in Blackfoot Indian Culture,* Bureau of American Ethnology Bulletin 159. Washington, 1955.

Grinnell, George Bird. *Blackfoot Lodge Tales.* New York, 1892.

Hungry Wolf, Adolf. *The Blood People.* Harper & Row, New York, 1977.

Hungry Wolf, Beverly. *The Ways of My Grandmothers.* Wm. Morrow & Co., New York, 1980.

McClintock, Walter. *The Old North Trail.* London, 1910.

Schaeffer, Claude. *Unpublished field notes on the Blackfoot Indians, ca. 1935-1960.* (American Museum of Natural History, New York, and Glenbow-Alberta Institute, Calgary.)

Schultz, James Willard. *Blackfeet and Buffalo.* University of Oklahoma Press, Norman, 1962.

— — —. *My Life as an Indian.* Boston, 1907.

Wissler, Clark. *The Social Life of the Blackfoot Indians.* American Museum of Natural History *Anthropological Papers,* Vol. VII, part 1, 1911.

BELOW: Duck Head, Chief of the Siksika, with his wife and horses, at a Sun Dance Camp, c. 1920.   (H. Pollard Photo - Provincial Museum and Archives of Alberta)

THE SARCEE TRIBE

Although by population they are the smallest native group in the Northern Rockies, the Sarcees are actually part of a very large Athapascan-speaking family that includes the Navajos of the southwestern U.S., who migrated from the north long ago. Their closest relatives are the Beaver Indians of northern Alberta, whose speech is nearly the same.

While the name Sarcee is not a word in that language, Sarcee people traditionally call themselves "Tsu T'inna," said to mean "Earth people," or "Many People," probably from back in the times when all Athapascans still lived close together. The Navajos in the south call themselves "Dineh," which is similar to "T'inna," while the far northern people have become known as the "Dene Nation."

Sarcee legends say they split from the main group one Winter, long ago, when a woman tried to pull up a buffalo horn frozen into the ice of a large lake that the whole group was crossing. The ice cracked and divided the lake in two, leaving part of the people north of it, the rest south. The latter group continued travelling southwards, away from their forested country, until they reached the buffalo plains, where they remained. Since then, the Sarcees have been known as hunters of the "xaniti," or buffalo.

This change from woods life to plains life happened slowly, as the people moved southward. By the late 1700's, Sarcee camps were often seen around the headwaters of the North Saskatchewan River, then later around the Beaver Hills.

The explorer Alexander Henry wrote around 1800: "These people have a reputation of being the bravest tribe in all the plains, who dare face ten times their own numbers, and of this I have had convincing proof during my residence in this country. They are more civilized and more closely attached to us than the Slaves (Blackfoot). . . Most of them have a smattering of the Cree language. . . their own language is so difficult to acquire that none of our people have ever learned it."

Early in this southward migration, the Sarcees established a good friendship with the Blackfoot Nation, whose members controlled the vast area into which the Sarcees were migrating. Together, they formed such a close alliance that they were often described as being another division of the four-member Blackfoot Confederacy.

Since the territory behind them was a domain of their Beaver relatives, this new alliance with the Blackfeet helped assure their survival on the hostile Plains, where enemy war parties sometimes came in much greater numbers than the Sarcees.

Around the year 1800, Sarcee population was estimated at 650 people living in ninety lodges. These were the survivors of several epidemics, including one of smallpox, twenty years earlier, that had cut the population down to below 300. Members of neighboring tribes helped swell the population through intermarriage, especially from among the Blackfoot people and somewhat from the Cree.

After rising to an estimated high of 800 people by 1836, the population tumbled back down to about 250 during another smallpox epidemic the following year. Recovery looked good at 420 when the next epidemic hit in 1869. This time there were less than 100 survivors; some thought the Sarcees were about to become extinct.

But the tribe has survived, continuing with its own heritage and culture. There were 255 people by the 1877 signing of Treaty Seven. At that time there were five bands within the tribe, led by the chiefs Big Plume, Bull Head, Little Drum, Many Horses, and Painted Otter.

In the treaty, a large land reserve was set aside for joint use by the Blackfoot, Bloods and Sarcees, The land bordered the Bow River, starting twenty miles upstream from Blackfoot Crossing and running down to the Red Deer River. A smaller part of this

ABOVE: A Sarcee Camping lodge, c. 1900   (Edward S. Curtis Photo)

ABOVE: A young Sarcee family, c. 1890 (C.W. Mathers Photo)

was later designated specifically for the Sarcees, starting three miles above Blackfoot Crossing, heading westward towards the mountains.

At that time there were still lots of buffalo, so the Sarcees gave little thought to settling on their reserved strip of land, most of which was virtually useless for farming, anyway. The year after the treaty signing found them camping and hunting for buffalo around Fort Macleod. In 1879 they moved up to their Reserve for a while, but after violent arguments with the Blackfoot they moved away again, following the last buffalo herds down into Montana.

Life changed greatly for the Sarcees beginning in the Spring of 1880, when government rations of beef and flour took the place of buffalo hunting, although small-scale hunting and wild plant gathering has continued right up to the present.

After accepting the reality of having to settle in just one place, the Sarcees insisted they wanted to live closer to the Rocky Mountains, by themselves. Troubles with the Blackfoot continued, so Chief Bull Head led his people to Fort Calgary, from where they made a tough Winter trip south to Fort Macleod, where rations were available.

In the Spring of 1881 they were forced to move back to their assigned area near Blackfoot Crossing, where land was to be plowed so that they could seed it for themselves.

When no plowing was done, Bull Head insisted the government give his people a different homeland, and this time he won.

A new treaty in 1883 gave the Sarcees one full Township, consisting of 108 square miles, including some prairie to cultivate and a lot of bushland to hunt, west of Fort Calgary, towards the Rocky Mountain foothills. By the end of that year they had built 33 log houses; in the next year they began growing their own crops. Wrote their agent: "Bull Head turned out, getting his people to work with a will. Quite a number asked to have separate gardens. . ."

Combining some hunting with the ability to grow their own food gave the Sarcees a fairly secure life, without the hardships of disappearing buffalo herds or sudden enemy attacks. In a short while their gardens were turning out good harvests that included 60 bushels of barley, 70 of turnips and 35 of potatoes. Those who wanted to earn cash were able to go into the nearby city of Calgary to sell wood, hay, horses, wild berries and tanned hides. Others found work on nearby ranches.

Unfortunately, the new life also brought much suffering from tuberculosis and other diseases, so that from 1880 into the 1920's the tribe's population steadily declined. In a typical year, there were 12 deaths and only 9 births. Also, the nearby city provided bootleg liquor and other demoralizing pastimes for those who became discouraged with reserve life.

Anglican missionaries came to the Sarcees with good intentions in 1886, though with practically no understanding of Sarcee spiritual and social values. Their efforts to remold the people in the "Christian" style of the period led to much frustration and disappointment on both sides. Wrote the Indian agent:

"To understand the difficulties to be contended with in dealing with the Sarcees, it must be remembered that they are more tenacious of their customs and superstitions than other Indians. . . Until recently they believed themselves doomed to extinction in the near future, and did not appear to wish to exert themselves to avoid what they considered to be their inevitable fate. . ."

A near-low in population was again reached in 1924, with only 160 people. But since that time the figures have shown a steady growth; a 1984 census lists 717, with statistics indicating better health and living conditions, so that the number can be expected to reach 1,000 before too many more years. The present Sarcee Reserve consists of 67,399 acres (27,276 hectares).

By the year 1900 several Sarcee families had borrowed government cattle to start small herds of their own in an effort to learn the ranching business. The tribal harvest in that year included 3,723 bushels of wheat, 1,300 bushels of root crops and 505 tons of hay. Big Crow, One Spot and Jim Big Plume became the first Sarcees to have their own mowing machines; in 1907, Crow Child became the first Sarcee to support himself on the reserve. By 1911 there were 304 head of Sarcee owned cattle.

In recent years, sources of income on the Sarcee Reserve have included cattle, oil and gas royalties, plus the Redwood Meadows Golf Course and townsite, a subdivision for non-tribe members. The Sarcee tribe has its own police force and social services, a museum. rodeo and campgrounds, plus a Sportsplex and Agriplex.

Traditional Sarcee Society

The Sarcee tribe in the past was made up of several bands that roamed and camped some distance apart from each other in their constant search for buffalo. Like other buffalo hunting people of the Plains, they lived in tipis and wore clothing made of tanned hides. In the late 1700's they switched from walking and using dogs for packing, to a life centred around horses.

Religion was a part of everything; all important activities were accompanied by prayers. Complex ceremonies guided the people through the cycle of annual seasons. Highest of these ceremonies was the mid-Summer Sun Dance, for which all the bands joined and celebrated together. Most ceremonies involved the use of medicine bundles, whose contents symbolized the sacredness of outdoor life. The bundles and ceremonies were nearly identical to those of the Blackfoot people, although Sarcee songs and language were always used.

BELOW: Sarcee Medicine Pipe ceremony, c. 1920
(Arnold Lupson Photo - Glenbow Alberta Institute)

ABOVE: Three young Sarcee wives, with dog travois, c. 1890   (C.W. Mathers Photo)

Sarcee bands were led by chiefs whose followers usually admired them and had faith in their abilities to find food and avoid dangers. People were free to choose whom they wanted to follow; band members and chiefs changed with time. The men all belonged to one of five warrior societies, from which they got strength to fight for and defend their people. Each society gave four-day ritual dances and ceremonies once a year, witnessed by the whole tribe. The group known as Painted Red was also the police force during the tribal Sun Dances.

A special headdress worn by the holy woman of the Sun Dance was kept with the tribe's main religious article, the Beaver Bundle. The men and women who took care of this were always very knowledegable about nature, keeping track of the seasons, learning many dances in imitation of the birds and animals whose preserved skins made up part of the bundle, knowing the special songs to accompany each one. This bundle is still in the tribe today.

Also still in the tribe is the most important of several Sarcee Medicine Pipe bundles, which were always cared for by chiefs and leaders, along with their wives. Rarely smoked, the pipes and contents of these bundles also required complex songs and ceremonies to bestow blessings on the tribe and its people.

Lodges that were covered with symbolic paintings were also handled with songs and rituals, like medicine bundles. The articles and ceremonies were ritually transferred from one family to another. At one time there were at least a dozen such painted lodges in Sarcee camps, each one having originated in the spiritual dreams of some respected person. The following is an example of such a dream, as told by a noted chief of the early 1900's.

"Old Sarcee" dreams of the Owl Lodge

"Once when I was a young man, travelling alone to another camp, I saw an owl sitting on its nest; I shot one of the young birds with my arrow. The mother bird disappeared over a hill, but presently returned with a hawk, which flew down to the edge of the creek near the wounded bird and struck its side with its wings. Moving over, it struck its other side, whereupon the young owl stretched out both its wings, healed. A third time the hawk struck it on the head; and a fourth, on the tail. Then both birds flew away and settled beside the mother owl. Immediately I found myself inside a painted tent like the one I now occupy, with the mother owl sitting beside me. She said to me 'If you had killed my child , you yourself would have died; but now that my child is healed I give you the privilege of erecting a tent like this one.' Many years after the vision I painted this tent."

46

Sarcee Bands and some of their families in 1921

1. **Blood Band;** also called **Big Plume's Band;** includes the families of Yellow Lodge, Dick Knight, Bull Collar, Peter Big Plume, Joe Big Plume, Jack Big Plume. Most families were of mixed Sarcee and Blood descent, giving origin to the band name.

2. **Broad Grass Band;** also called **Tents Cut Down,** or **Crow Child's Band;** includes the families of Crow Child, Bertie Crow Child, Sleigh, Many Wounds, and Peter Many Wounds. Said to be of mixed Sarcee and Cree descent, the name referring to long, broad grass growing up north.

3. **People who hold aloof (natsistina);** also called **Crow Chief's Band;** includes families of Charlie Crow Chief, Tony, Wolf, Otter, Oscar Otter, Pat Grasshopper (senior and junior) and Bob Left Hand. Considered mostly pure Sarcee.

4. **Uterus Band;** also called **Old Sarcee's Band;** includes families of Old Sarcee, One Spot, David One Spot, Fox Tail, Two Young Men, Tom Heaven Fire, Two Guns, Crow Collar, George Big Crow, Dick Starlight, Jim Starlight, Sarcee Woman, Young Bull Head, Dodging Horse, and Anthony Dodging Horse. Many were of mixed Sarcee and Blackfoot descent.

5. **Young Buffalo Robe Band,** also called **Many Horses' Band,** or **"Those who keep together."** Includes families of Tom Many Horses, Big Knife, Running in the Middle, Dog, and John Waters. Mostly considered pure Sarcee.

From "Sarcee Indians", by Diamond Jenness

BELOW: The family of Sarcee Chief Big Belly, including his wife Maggie (right), daughter Mary (One Spot, center), and his mother-in-law, a Blood woman (left).
(Arnold Lupson Photo, Glenbow-Alberta Institute)

ABOVE: Sarcee head chief Big Belly, also a noted medicine man, c. 1915

(H. Pollard Photo - Alberta Provincial Museum and Archives)

SARCEE HEAD CHIEFS

Bull Head	c.	1870 - 1911
Big Belly		1913 - 1920
Joe Big Plume		1921 - 1946
David Crowchild		1947 - 1952
James Starlight		1953 - 1966
Dick Big Plume		1966 - 1970
Clifford Big Plume		1976 - 1984
Roy Whitney		1984 - 1986
Clifford Big Plume		1986 - 1988
Roy Whitney		1988 -

Sarcee General Calendar

January - February	= "Old Man Moon"
February - March	= "Moon White", meaning White-headed Eagle.
March - April	= "Duck Moon"
May - June	= "Frog Moon"
June - July	= "Birds come out of Nest"
July - August	= "Mid-year without Snow Moon"
August - September	= "Ripening Berries Moon"
September - October	= "Leaves Falling Moon"
October - November	= "Elk sits down in the Creek"
November - December	= "Mid-year with Snow Moon"

Seasonal Cycle

Winter: Groups of several families camped along the edge of the woods at distances of one or two day's journey apart.

Early Spring (when buffalo began to come north); These groups moved out on the open prairies to hunt and replenish stocks of food, leather and robes.

Summer (when many buffalo herds roamed the plains and many wild plants could be harvested): Numerous small parties, even single families, hunted separately a few miles apart. Once or occasionally twice in the season the entire tribe united to drive the herds of buffalo into a pound or to force them over a cliff. This was the usual season for visiting the trading posts, though in some years visits were made in Winter.

Late Summer: The tribe united for the society dances and the Sun Dance.

Early Autumn: The tribe dispersed again into groups, which gradually retreated to the edge of the woods. This was the favorite season also, for raids on neighbouring tribes.

Sarcee Land

Although the Sarcee Reserve is rather small, its location so near the city of Calgary has caused great pressure on the tribe for sales of its lands, which the people and their chiefs have steadfastly opposed. The Canadian government leased 11,800 acres of the reserve starting in 1903, for use as the Sarcee military camp, although this land was returned to the tribe recently after the base was closed. In 1931, the tribe surrendered 593.5 acres for the Glenmore Reservoir, while the Department of National Defence got 940 acres in 1952.

Back in 1913, head chief Big Belly had this to say about selling Sarcee land:

"We won't sell our land. The white man have all the land; he has taken it from the Indians. All we are left with is one small piece and now he wants it and will leave us with none. I say no, we won't sell."

Sarcee Bibliography

Sarcee Culture Program, "Tsu T'ina."
Dempsey, Hugh, "The Sarcee Indians," Glenbow paper Vol. 4 No. 5, 1971.
Lupson, Arnold, "The Sarcee," Glenbow Museum and Archives papers.
Jenness, Diamond, "Sarcee Indians".

ABOVE: Traditional Sarcee food preparations, c. 1900. (Edward S. Curtis Photo)

THE STONEY TRIBE

Nakoda is the name that Stoneys call themselves, which means "the People." They speak the same kind of Siouan language as their famous distant relatives, the Lakota, better known as the Sioux.

Stoneys are more directly related to neighbors of the Sioux, the Assiniboine. Tribal legends say the first groups of Stoneys left their larger Assiniboine family on the central Plains during a smallpox outbreak in the 1600's. At that time the Assiniboines were a major force on the Plains, with several thousand warriors.

The bands now known as Stoneys were never very large, made up mostly of families related to each other by blood or marriage. They braved great dangers in migrating across the Plains to seek new homelands. Those who ended up in the Rocky Mountains also changed their lifestyles, from complete dependence on buffalo to the mountain life of hunting elk, moose, deer and sheep, with buffalo becoming only an occasional highlight. This change helped assure Stoney survival; as small groups they remained relatively sheltered in the mountains, while on the open plains they might have been easily wiped out by much larger groups of enemies.

By the early 1800's it was estimated there were between ten and thirty thousand Assiniboine people altogether, though accurate counts were impossible, since the many bands were widely scattered, more so than most other tribes. Two groups of them were recorded as "Stone Indians" on an early map, which showed one group living along the Battle River in Saskatchewan, the other between the North Saskatchewan River and the Pembina.

When Stoneys went out on the prairies for occasional buffalo hunts, they often did so in the company of Cree friends, with whom they usually got along. Early written accounts of Stoneys are sometimes confused by these friendships. Although Stoneys may have been in the Rockies long before 1808, a report written at Fort Vermilion around that time mentioned only two groups of Assiniboines living that far west, the Swampy Ground Assiniboines and the Strong Wood Assiniboines. Head chief of the latter group was Old Star, a Kootenay who had been captured as a boy and raised as a Stoney. Old Star's Stoney descendants today carry the family name Kootenay.

Tribal history tells of two Assiniboine bands that came west to the mountains and split up, one reaching the foothills around Chief Mountain, the other going much further north to enter the foothills near modern-day Jasper National Park, in the area of the Red Deer and North Saskatchewan Rivers. The northern group eventually became known as the Wesley Band of Stoney Indians, while the southern group split up into the Bearspaw and Chiniki Bands.

The southern group used a series of campgrounds along the Eastern Slopes and Front Ranges of the Rockies, including the upper reaches of the Oldman, Highwood, Sheep, Bow and Ghost Rivers. In the 1850's it was estimated that some 2,000 Stoneys roamed Alberta's foothills.

It is often thought Stoneys are named for their life in the Rocky Mountains, but tribal historians say the name was first given by white explorers because of the method used for making native broth.

Before Europeans brought pots and kettles, Indians used a different method for bringing water to a boil. They would dig a hole in the ground about the size of a bucket, which they lined with a clean, wet rawhide. Into this they put pieces of meat and wild vegetables, along with water. From a nearby fire they brought small, round stones which were very hot; these were dropped into the rawhide bowl, quickly bringing the water to a boil without burning through the rawhide. Before long, the food was cooked soft

ABOVE: Stony Camp on the Bow River, c. 1900   (Edward S. Curtis Photo)

and a hot broth was ready. From this process the old Nakoda say they became known as Stoneys.

Dwellings in those days were not only the buffalo hide tipis used by other Plains tribes, but also tipi shaped lodges covered in the summer by spruce bark and in the winter by layers of moss, small poles, clay and mud. The three Stoney bands wintered separately along the Bow River, the Highwood River and up at the Kootnenay Plains.

European trade goods improved the quality of traditional Stoney life, though the same cannot be said about the arrival of Europeans themselves. Nevertheless, Stoney chiefs and leaders welcomed them and have remained on friendly terms ever since. There have been no major fights or battles between the two during more than 150 years of direct relationships.

Traders and explorers were the first Europeans to meet Stoneys, beginning in the late 1700's. But it was not until the later 1800's that outsiders actually came to settle among the tribe. These were missionaries, whose good intentions were limited by an absolute belief that Indians should give up their own ways of life and learn to be like the newcomers.

Wesleyan missionary Robert Rundle was the first of these preachers, arriving in 1840 and remaining for eight years. Some of the people welcomed him with respect, while others had little to do with him, going about their traditional life far from his influence. But when the Rev. George McDougall came in 1863, he brought plans to establish his whole family among the Stoneys in order to convert them into practitioners of the Bible. Like others, this man came with good intentions, but he looked at Stoney ways only through his European eyes.

To begin with, he wanted all three bands to live together as a single tribe, in one place. With his son, the Rev. John McDougall, he established the Morleyville mission in the centre of Stoney country, along the Bow River. Although Morley has been like a Stoney capitol ever since, individual family groups and bands continued to wander up and down the foothills to camp and hunt for many more years.

When Treaty Seven was signed in 1877, the Stoneys placed their future in the hands of the McDougalls, who were their trusted advisors and interpreters. They thought these spiritual leaders were working for the Creator and for the Stoney people, without realizing or understanding the wider view of the McDougalls' long-range interests, to see Western Canada settled, civilized and Christian. Having the Stoneys settle in one area was only a small step towards the larger goal.

Bearspaw, Chiniki and Jacob Goodstoney signed Treaty Seven as head chiefs of the three main Stoney bands. The councillors who signed with them included Abraham and Patrick Bigstoney, George Crawler, James Dixon and George Twoyoungmen, There were 501 people listed as "Mountain Stonies," though not everyone in the tribe attended the treaty signing; many were opposed to the conditions.

Treaty negotiators wanted to have one chief speak for all the Stoneys, favoring Chiniki, who spoke both Stoney and Cree. But this went against their customs, so the people did not approve. Furthermore, those who were mainly from the north or south did not want to settle around Morley, which was considered Chiniki country. As a result, the original Stoney Indian Reserve was mainly surveyed on the advice of Chief Chiniki and Rev. John McDougall, who had his home, farm and church well established at that place.

But even Chief Chiniki was disappointed by the treaty, which gave the Stoneys a much smaller area than he had asked for. In addition, government promises were said to be like sacred words, although later some of them were broken, leading to much distrust among Stoneys for outsiders.

ABOVE: Stony Chiefs in the early 1900's. From left to right: Hector Crawler; Jonas Twoyoungmen; Jacob Bearspaw; Peter Wesley; Amos Bigstoney; Joshua Mark. (Archives of the Canadian Rockies, Banff)

In 1885 the Canadian Pacific Railway was built through the Stoney Reserve, on its way from Coast to Coast, thus bringing "civilization" to the tribe almost overnight. Outsiders came, taking minerals and trees, fencing the land and hunting the wild animals mainly for "trophies." Mountain hunting had helped the Stoneys remain fairly independent while their prairie neighbors were forced to rely on government rations, after the buffalo were gone. But soon wildlife became harder to find even in the mountains, while the creation of Banff and Jasper National Parks restricted Stoneys from some of their best hunting trails. Since crops did not grow well in their reserve's rocky soil, either, Stoneys became forced to depend on government rations, as well.

About ten years after the railroad came, a new band formed behind the noted Stoney leader, Peter Wesley, also known as Moosekiller. He took about 100 people from Jacob's Band and moved north to their traditional hunting area around the Kootenay Plains. This was against government prohibitions, which required Indians to obtain passes in order to leave their Reserves. "Wandering the land" otherwise was subject to punishment for vagrancy. Ever since 1895, Stoneys leaders have battled government bureaucracy (both federal and provincial) to obtain a permanent reserve for this group, although 5,000 acres was allotted to them in 1947, forming the Bighorn Reserve.

In 1918 part of the Bearspaw Band also moved away from Morley, back south to their traditional hunting area, around the Highwood River. This group spent the next 25 years living semi-nomadic, as in the past, hunting along their old trails and working for various ranchers to obtain a little money. A 5,000 acre ranch was finally purchased in 1946 and established as the Eden Valley Reserve.

Some Stoney Place Names

Place names in Stoney country often depended on personal experiences, so they varied among different family groups and time periods. For instance, a popular campsite might be named by one group for a noted horse that they lost, by another for a good hunt, by a third for an enemy attack they survived there. The following list, therefore, is given mainly to record some examples.

Bow River: Bow wood was commonly cut along its banks. The common Stoney name today is *"Cold River."*

Bragg Creek: Western stretches are called *"Round Clearing Creek";* this "Round Clearing" was a very popular Stoney campground. Eastern stretches are called *"Crackling River,"* for the sounds of its waters.

Brazeau River: *"Big Fork"*

Calgary: *"Elbow City."*

Canmore: *"Shooting at what looked like an animal in the Willows,"* from an event in which a Stoney hunter was fooled by dim lighting. Nearby campground called *"Round Clearing";* later known as *"Indian Flats."*

Cascade Mountain: *"Minay Rhappa."*

Cataract Creek: *"No Fish River."*

Crowsnest River: *"Two Old Men River."*

Elbow River: *"Crackling River,"* from the sound of its many rapids.

Exshaw: *"Place with many Stumps,"* so named after Stoneys cut the trees to sell as firewood to the nearby Lime Pit operations, leaving a stubble of stumps.

Fish Creek: *"Decayed Wood Creek;"* also *"Muddy Creek"* and *"Where the Black-Brownish Coloured Horse Died."*

Highwood River: *"Tall Trees River,"* from the tall aspen groves along its banks.

Jumping Pound Creek: *"Where a Blackfoot Woman was brought Home;"* also called *"Where the Blackfoot Camped"* or *"Where a Blackfoot was Clubbed."*

Kananaskis River: *"Y-shaped Fork,"* referring to the fork joining the Bow River with the Kananaskis. Also called *"Spirit Waters,"* because it ran so clear.

Upper Kananaskis Lake: *"Lake at the Forks."*

Lake Minnewanka: *"Spirit Lake"* (Minnay-wanka).

Livingstone Creek: *"Buffalo Head Creek."* named for a noted Stoney elder named Buffalo Head, who used to live by the large pond at its headwaters, *"Buffalo Head Lake,"* now named **Buffalo Lake.**

Moose Mountain: *"Mountain by Itself."*

Mount Allan: *"Grizzly Hill;"* also called *"Burnt Timber Hill."*

Nihahi Creek: One of the few places officially known by its Stoney name, which means *"Ravine Creek."*

Rocky Mountain House: *"Old House."*

Sheep River: Same name in Stoney, because the steep cliffs along it were favored by Mountain Sheep.

Spray Lakes: *"Where Fish were netted and trapped."* A favorite Stoney fishing place.

ABOVE: A Stony camp in the Rocky Mountain foothills of Alberta, c. 1899.

(Edward S. Curtis Photo)

Stoney Calendar

Spring: *"Everything off the Ground."*
Summer: *"Everything Green."*
Autumn: *"Everything turns to yellow."*
Fall: *"First snow."*
Winter: *"Nothing but snow."*

January: *"Middle Moon Brother"*
February: *"Middle Moon"*
March: *"Golden Eagle Moon"*
April: *"Goose Moon"*
May: *"Golden Eagle Moon"*
June: *"Grass Moon"*
July: *"Red Berries Moon"*
August: *"Elk-in-heat Moon"*
September: *"Moose Breeding Moon"*
October: *"Half-Summer, half-Winter Moon"*
November: *"Frost on Trees Moon"*
December: *"Breeding Moon"*

Stoney Reserve Lands

Morley = 96,699 acres (39,134 hectares)
North of Morley = 14,026 acres (5,678 hectares)
Bighorn = 5,257 acres (2,127 hectares)
Eden Valley = 4,178 acres (1,690 hectares)

Stoneys Today

The 1984 census lists 2,382 Stoneys, 802 for the Chiniki Band, 807 for the Bearspaw and 773 for the Wesley. Living on the edge of poverty for many years, the tribe has finally been able to improve its own situation with the help of income from gas wells drilled on Reserve lands. At the same time, there are now many well-educated tribe members capable of handling modern business, schooling and administration.

As part of building its own economic base, the Stoney tribe has developed a number of service and tourist-oriented businesses, including sawmills, gas stations, a cement-mixing plant, restaurants, camping facilities and handicraft shops. The lakeside Nakoda Lodge Conference Centre has attracted world-wide attention from prestigious groups. It includes the Nakoda Institute Research and Learning Centre, which emphasizes the continuation of Stoney culture.

The Stoneys are admired by many tribes because of the way they have managed to keep alive their own language and culture. Many Stoney children start out life knowing only their native language; among Stoney adults, most men still do some hunting, women still tan hides and do beadwork. Well-attended pow-wows are held throughout the year, while every Summer sees the erection of one or more Sun Dance lodges, testimonials to a surviving faith in Nature among the Stoneys even though their lands are crossed by paved highways, railways, factories, power dams and endless streams of people.

Stony Indian Camp, Calgary

ABOVE: Bow River and Calgary in background, 1888.

(Howard & Chapman Photo, Victoria)

SOME STONY HEAD CHIEFS
(with approximate year served)

BEARSPAW BAND:
Bearspaw (c. 1877)
Johnny Bearspaw (c. 1957)
Jonas Rider
Bill Ear Sr.
Una Wesley 1984 (first woman Chief)

CHINIKI BAND:
John Chiniki 1870's - 1905
Jonas TowYoungMen 1906 - 1911
Hector Crawler
Frank Powderface 1979

WESLEY BAND:
Goodstoney 1870's
Jacob 1890's
Moosekiller (Peter Wesley) 1890's
Enos Hunter (1940's and 1950's)
Tom Snow   1949 - 1955
Tom Kaquitts 1967 - 1968
John Snow   1969 -

Stoney Bibliography

Barbeau, Marius, "Indian Days on the Western Prairies,," National Museum of Canada, 1959.
Barbeau, Marius, "Indian Days in the Canadian Rockies;" Macmillan of Canada, Toronto, 1923.
Chiniki Research Team, "Stoney Place Names."
Jonker, Peter M., "Stoney Historical Notes."
Lowie, Robert H., "The Assiniboine," Anthropological Papers.
American Museum of Natural History, Vol. IV, 1909.
Snow, Chief John, "My Stoney People."

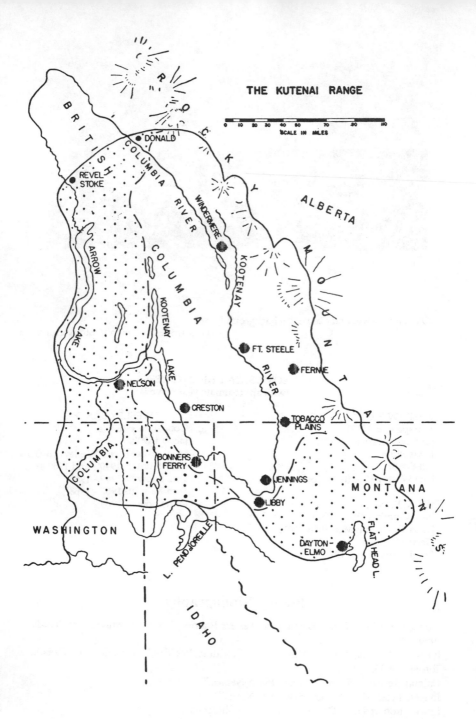

THE KUTENAI RANGE

SCALE IN MILES

BRITISH COLUMBIA

DONALD

REVEL-
STOKE

ROCKY

ALBERTA

WINDERMERE

KOOTENAY

COLUMBIA RIVER

ARROW LAKE

KOOTENAY LAKE

MOUNTA

FT. STEELE

FERNIE

NELSON

CRESTON

TOBACCO
PLAINS

COLUMBIA

BONNERS
FERRY

JENNINGS

MONTANA

LIBBY

WASHINGTON

L. PEND OREILLE

DAYTON-
ELMO

FLAT HEAD L.

IDAHO

Kootenay Origins

Elderly Kootenay Indians in the late 1800s said their ancestors came from an underground hole on the east side of the Rockies. That may be so, since ethnographers have been unable to discover other origins for the tribe. Even linguists cannot connect the Kootenay language with any other; it remains a linguistical island.

Kootenay, Kootenai, or Kutenai, the spelling makes little difference to tribal history, since everything was handed down orally; there was no writing. The word is spelled with a "u" in the United States, and with double "o" in Canada. It is generally pronounced "koot-knee." No one is sure where this name comes from, since it is not a word in the Kootenay language. Traditionally, Kootenay people spoke of themselves as, "a man of the Tobacco Plains Band," or "a woman of the Columbia Lakes Band." However, places like Tobacco Plains and Columbia Lakes also had their own Kootenay names, which came out very differently.

"Base Camp" for all Kootenay Indians has generally been Tobacco Plains, a small, mountain-ringed valley at the Canada-U.S. border, at the western foot of the Rockies. From here the people wandered, by small family groups as well as in large bands, along trails and waterways in northwest Montana, northern Idaho, southeast British Columbia, and the buffalo prairies of southwest Alberta. Until the late 1890's, almost all members of the tribe gathered once a year—usually at Tobacco Plains—for religious festivals, especially their version of the widely-practiced Sun Dance.

Many tribes lived a nomadic existence, like the Kootenays, with members scattering out in smaller groups to hunt and gather. With the reservation system of the later 1800s most Indians were gathered and settled in large tribal groups. The Kootenays are among a minority who received much smaller reservations, one for each of its scattered bands, generally in the camping area where they happened to be located. As with all North American Indian tribes, there is a great deal of controversy surrounding the history of Kootenay reservations and land claims.

Kootenay culture reflects the people's unique geographic position, with fishing people to the west and buffalo hunters east. As recently as one hundred years ago, virtually all Kootenay people still made their living by hunting and fishing, both. True, buffalo on the plains were wiped out by then—Kootenay hunters got their last ones in 1880—but the rugged Kootenay mountain and valley country had plenty of deer, elk and moose to subsist on.

Preference for either fishing or buffalo hunting divided the Kootenay tribe, or nation, into two harmonious segments. The so-called "Upper Kootenay" lived closer to the Rocky Mountains, kept larger horse herds, and made trips to the Plains once or twice a year for buffalo. Their surplus buffalo and horses were then traded to "Lower Kootenay" relatives, who preferred canoes over horses, staying near home waters to trap fish, spear salmon, and hunt small game, including ducks and geese.

A Kootenay Historical Record

From Chief Paul David

Certain Kootenay people were noted as keepers of tribal history, which was passed down orally, mostly at the campfires. The historians used certain tricks to help them recall past events. Notches were made on special sticks, or on hide scrapers made of elkhorn. Some tied knots on special cords, sometimes adding beads for peculiar events.

The following historical record is handed down from Hollow Head, a Kootenay born in 1879. On a piece of hide, he kept a set of symbols and signs which served to remind him of various events. Chief Paul David learned this record from Hollow Head some time before the latter's death in 1906. He gave a copy of this record to Dr. Claude E. Schaeffer in the summer of 1935.

Three circles at the start of this historical record represent the first three years in Hollow Head's life, during which he knew of no peculiar incidents.

OOO

The next nine circles indicate the number of years Kanuktutam, "White Hair," had his fur trading camp at Jennings, Montana. The seventh circle has a vertical line representing an eclipse of the Sun. Hollow Head used a triangle to represent the trader's camp.

After this, the same trader moved camp to *Aganoho*, "Tobacco Plains." (Chief Paul David thought this Aganoho meant the Kutenai term for bird.)

A line on the next symbol represents some division within Hollow Head's band, while the dot represents an important birth, although the exact details are forgotten.

| •

The three dots represent important births, but again the details are lost.

• ▪ •

Six circles indicate the number of years a trader named "Twisted Nose" camped at Libby. The campsite is recalled by an M-shaped symbol. This was from 1834 to 1840.

The next five years were spent mainly at a campsite near Waldo, B.C. called *Gamuqvki*, represented by the first symbol. The cross on the second circle stands for the first Catholic sermon delivered to the Kutenais. The cross and curved line over the next circle refers to the arrival of Father De Smet. This was in the year 1845.

For the next two years the band wintered at a place near Libby called *Gatskai-amina*. Two dots represent the years, while a curve represents Libby's location on the Kootenai River. The last symbol indicates two buttes which loomed over the campsite.

The next two winters were spent at *Wawayukma*, "Curled-brim hat."

The next three years were spent near Tobacco Plains. The cross between the second and third dot represents the birth of Chief Paul David in 1852.

BELOW: Chief Paul David in 1931, near Grasmere, B.C. A noted historian and ceremonial leader, he succeeded his father as chief of the Tobacco Plains band in 1891

This year is noted for the arrival of the trader *Suyvpvnana*, "Young White Man," who built a trading post at "Hairy Prairie" along the Flathead River in B.C., where Chief Paul David's band wintered.

This is the year 1855, when the mission at St. Eugene was founded. All the band moved there for baptism and marriage, except that some individuals camped with the trader Suyvpvnana. The circle with four prongs recalls the Kutenai chief Bull Robe, who was killed this year in a battle. Gov. Stevens came to make a treaty with the Kutenai, this summer.

This year the band again wintered at Wawayukma.

For four years the band wintered at Haydon, which is symbolized by a banner with four triangles. Suyvpvnana was the resident trader. During this time a government official came to see about the International Boundary line. The Kutenais misunderstood him and thought he was going to cut their country literally in two, so that relatives would not see each other again.

Winter camp for the next four years was at Gateway, shown by an oval with six legs. Suyvpvnana was again the resident trader, but he sold out and moved west during the fourth year, marked by a line.

In this year, Michael Phillips arrived as trader to the Kutenais. He married into the tribe and spent the rest of his life there. His discovery of coal led to Crowsnest Pass mining developments. Through all these years traders offered Kutenais about the same basic items, such as guns, knives, awls, pots and so forth, although the posts were moved from place to place.

For the next four years Michael Phillips ran the trading post, while the Kutenais wintered with him. A Mr. Hardisty took over the post in the fifth year; he is represented by a circle with two prongs. The large circle with two dots is said to represent a campsite on a large prairie with two pine forests in the middle.

This dotted circle with a tail refers to the first winter during which all the Kutenai bands did not winter together with the trader, but each wintered separately.

The Y represents an important summer during which peace was made with three of the Blackfoot divisions — Bloods, North Piegan and Montana Blackfeet. This was in 1875.

Y

In this year Paul David's band wintered at a place he called "Pine Prairie," where the Kutenai head chief Michelle died. The tilted cross represents this event.

The band again wintered at "Pine Prairie," which was in the area of Tobacco Plains. Highlight of the year came "when the earth moved," the result of an earthquake felt in many parts of the northern Rockies.

This circle marks the last time that Chief Paul David's band wintered away from Tobacco Plains, about 1878. After this they wintered around Eureka, Montana, until the mid-1880s, after which they settled on the Tobacco Plains Reserve, at Grasmere, B.C., just over the International line.

BELOW: Upper Kootenay family, at the foot of the B.C. Rockies, c. 1880.

White Man's History of the Kootenays

Collected by Dr. Claude E. Schaeffer

October, 1800: Explorer David Thompson makes first recorded contact between whites and Kootenays, bringing a trading party of Indians back with him to Rocky Mountain House, west of present-day Edmonton, Alberta.

Later that same month, Le Blanc and La Gasse, French-Canadian "engages," cross the Rocky Mountains with these Kootenays to winter and trap in their country. They stay for several years, each summer returning to Rocky Mountain House with furs, some of which they trapped, some they purchased from Kootenay Indians. Their stay ends when one of the pair is killed on suspicion of having guided a Stoney war party to a secluded Kootenay camp, in which several people are left dead.

1801: David Thompson and James Hughes make an unsuccessful attempt to cross the Rocky Mountains to Kootenay country.

1806: John MacDonald of Garth sends Jaco Finley and other men to cut a trail across the Rockies to the Columbia River, in Kootenay country.

1807: David Thompson, with three men and an Indian guide, crosses the Rockies to build Kootanae House on the west side of the Columbia River at Lake Windermere.

1808: On April 20, after all the ice is gone, David Thompson leaves Lake Windermere on a trading expedition south. Descending the Kootenay River from where it meets Columbia Lake (at Canal Flats), he travels to Bonner's Ferry, where he meets a combined camp of Kootenays and Flatheads (this time at peace, though often the two tribes fought). After more travelling he gets back to the Kootenay River at Fort Steele. From here he goes up the Wild Horse and Sheep Rivers, along the western foot of the Rockies, until he gets back to Kootanae House on June 5. This is thought to have been the first time a white man travelled around the whole Kootenay country.

1809: In spring, after the ice is gone, David Thompson heads down the Columbia River and across the Divide to Rocky Mountain House, having spent another winter collecting furs and trading with Indians at Kootanae House, on Windermere Lake. A smaller trading post had also operated that winter further south, at the falls of the Kootenay, under Finan McDonald, Thompson's assistant.

That fall, Thompson again crosses the Divide, heading upstream on the Columbia, then down the Kootenay, until he reaches the Great Road of the Flatheads at Bonner's Ferry. He travels south to Lake Pend d'Oreille, at the mouth of Clark's Fork River, meeting a large camp of Indians. He builds Kullyspel House on the east side of the lake. Leaving an assistant in charge of this, he moves on to a place later known as Woodlin, where he builds Saleesh House. At these three trading posts, built by David Thompson, the Kootenays innocently began trading in their ancient, self-sufficient lifestyle for manufactured goods like knives, cooking pots and axes.

1810: After again bringing furs to Rocky Mountain House, Thompson is prevented from making his usual crossing of the Divide by warriors of the Blackfoot Confederacy, angry because he has been trading rifles to their enemies, the Kootenay. To get around them, he finds a new trail, via Athabasca Pass, which he crosses with dogs and sleds at the end of December.

Thompson continues to explore Kootenay country and trade with surrounding tribes over the next few years. His work is later carried on by others whose principal purpose is to obtain furs from Indians in trade for material goods. Some of these traders are good, some are bad. Several marry Kootenay women and father children who stay with the tribe. Indians and mixed-bloods from the east also come to settle in the less populated west, trading with local Indians and introducing Christian ideas, along with European skills such as gardening and log house building.

1833: A letter written on July 29 from Capt. Bonneville to Major General Alex Macomb (?), says, "The Cottenais, 700 warriors, having the other day commenced a war with the Blackfoot, have been driven from their original grounds upon the Northern Branches of Columbia, and have now joined the Flatheads."

1842: Famous Catholic priest, Father De Smet, meets Kootenays for first time at Flathead lake.

1845: Father De Smet returns, also visits Tobacco Plains this time. Many Kootenays profess faith in his teachings.

1854: James Sinclair, who first passed through Kootenay country in 1841, leads another party through in this year. They enter via Kananaskis Pass, go down Palliser River to the Kootenay River, and down it to Tobacco Plains. Along the way they trade cattle for Kootenay horses.

1855: In July, delegates from the Kootenay people join Flatheads and Pend d'Oreilles at Council Grove, near Missoula, Montana, to meet Governor I.I. Stevens, representing the U.S. government, and to sign the important "Treaty of 1855," establishing permanent Kootenay claim to U.S. territory.

1857: The Kootenays get their first church, a small log chapel built by them at Fort Kootenay, with the guidance of a visiting priest.

1858: More noted explorers pass through Kootenay country. Captain Palliser comes via Kananaskis Pass, finds many Indian camps in the Kootenay River valley, then heads east again through Kootenay Pass. His compatriot, Dr. Hector, crosses the Rockies via Howse Pass, meets Kootenay families drying salmon at Columbia Lake, and leaves one of the earliest written descriptions of the tribe.

1859: International Boundary Commission taken down the Kootenay River this year by Chief Abraham.

1863: Gold found on Finlay Creek (above the Kootenay River) by Finlay brothers, who bring samples to Fort Kootenay, at Lake Windermere. A traveller takes one sample to Fort Colville, in Washington, from where news of the find spreads quickly, creating a gold rush into Kootenay country. Even better gold prospects found on Wild Horse Creek, above Fort Steele, where a thousand white miners are digging by 1865. A frontier mining town springs up, with ferry service across the Kootenay River provided by Galbraith brothers. An estimated fifteen million dollars in gold taken from the Wild Horse diggings.

1864: Edwin L. Bonner operates ferry and trading post among Lower Kutenai until 1876, then Richard Fry until 1892.

1865: Completion of the Dewdney Trail links Upper Kootenay country with the outside world. Chief Justice Baillie comes out from Victoria to show miners that law prevails. By 1869, the easy gold is gone, along with most of the miners and other people. A few Chinese stay on to rework the old diggings.

1874: Canadian customs moved from Wild Horse to Joseph's Prairie, with new headquarters built by Michael Phillips. John Galbraith opens a store nearby, and starts a ranch. Later, Col. James Baker buys the ranch and names the place Cranbrook. He orders Kootenays to vacate the land, but they claim rights from prior settlement. As more settlers arrive, Kootenays finally decide to move to a quieter area around Fort Steele.

1882: W.A. Baillie-Grohman arrives with big plans to develop Kootenay country, though he finds only eleven settlers, most of them living near the Wild Horse mining camp. This camp also boasts a government official who acts as gold commissioner as well as constable; a postmaster; storekeeper; plus one Catholic missionary in charge of the Indian school and mission on St. Mary's River.

Noting the country's isolation because of poor land routes (the new Dewdney Trail was already completely blocked by fallen timber), Baillie-Grohman offers to build a steamboat canal, at Canal Flats, to connect the Kootenay and Columbia waterways, at the same time diverting floodwaters from potential farmland along the lower Kootenay reaches, if the B.C. Government gives him control over 48,000 acres of Kootenay land! Baillie-Grohman probably meant well, in his cultivated European way of thinking, but all odds were against him and the scheme eventually failed.

1888: Building of St. Eugene's Mission School, and government surveying of Kootenay reserves, officially ends free use by the Indian people of their ancestral country, with settlers putting up fences and buildings here and there. Still, several more generations of Kootenays spent at least part of every year camping in the old hunting and fishing grounds, visiting relatives from other bands along the way.

1898: Transportation changes in Kootenay country with the arrival of Canadian Pacific Railway tracks through Crowsnest Pass, coming from Lethbridge and the C.P.R. mainline at Medicine Hat. Travel along most of the Kootenay River still limited to steamboat, or adjacent wagon roads often impassable to anything with wheels.

1914: On December 11th, the first through passenger train steamed up the Kootenay Central Railway from a point near Cranbrook to Golden, bringing the mechanical world to the last big, wild valley in Kootenay country. It was then possible for Columbia Lake Kootenays to board a train at the Windermere station and ride for a visit to the St. Mary's Band or, with a change of trains at Cranbrook and other places, to almost all the other Kootenay bands on both sides of the International boundary.

BELOW: Kootenay camp in the Windermere Valley.

(Canadian Pacific Corporate Archives)

ABOVE: Chief Francis Francois, leader of the St. Mary's band, with some of his Upper Kootenay people, near Fort Steele, c. 1880.

Kootenay Campsites
in Montana, Idaho and British Columbia

Collected by Claude E. Schaeffer
from Chief Paul David and other Kootenay elders

1. *Vksuvk.* A prairie on the north side of the Kootenai River, near the highway bridge, northeast of **Libby, Montana**. The main wintering site of the *Akiyinik*. Families assembled here in July also for games, ceremonies and trade. Game and berries were plentiful while the river served as a partial barrier to enemy attack.

2. *Akii*, "Thigh Bone" An important winter site at the junction of Fisher and Kootenai Rivers near **Libby**. The Sun dance ceremony was once held here, long ago.

3. *Gomnini*, "Sleepy Place." A camp site east of the junction of Wolf Creek and Fisher River. Good hunting of blacktail and whitetail deer in this region.

4. *Aquanak Atamuko*, "Planting Place." An extensive prairie (also called Elk Prairie) where the Akayinik camped in summer to plant tobacco.

5. *Niltukp*, "Home of Antelope." A large campsite, the present **Pleasant Valley**. People from as far as Columbia Lakes and Tobacco Plains gathered Camas here. The site of a mythical race between Antelope and Frog.

6. *Kintankitska*, "Upper Fish Trap.' A fishing site on the south bank of Ashley Creek, a short distance east of **Athens, Montana**. In May a large trap was built here for fish moving upstream during freshet period. Often, a second trap was set farther down the creek.

7. *Yakakisvnka Miki*, "Two Pits in the Ground." An important winter site during the pre-reservation period. It was located between the Flathead River and the city of Kalispel. The Grizzly ceremony was frequently given here.

8. *Akvkmma Nam*, "Crossing Place." A summer camping place along Bitterroot Creek, on Bull-Robe's allotment. Bitterroot grew here in abundance and was gathered during the pre-reservation period.

9. *Akinmukupmat*, "Place where Coyote Cooked." A campsite on Chief Kustata's land, above Bitterroot Creek. Camas was abundant here. The term refers to a low knoll nearby where Coyote was said to have roasted camas. In gathering season the men gambled here while women gathered wild roots.

10. *Yakithat witnvmki*, "Place of Dancing." One of the campsites, a few miles from **Belton, Montana**, on the trail leading across the Rockies. The Blacktail Deer dance was frequently given here.

11. *Yakantvmkonamnvmki*, "Human Skull on a Stick." Located near the entrance of Canyon Creek. The term refers to the discovery of an enemy's skull here long ago.

12. *Akapatanana*, "Small piece of Animal Fat." A term applied to the region about the mouth of Warland Creek. There was good mountain sheep hunting between here and the following site.

13. *Akanuxo*, "Swift Current." An old and important winter site of the Upper Kutenai. It was situated on the lower Tobacco River, at the mouth of Graves Creek.

14. *Aquanak Alamuko*, "Planting Place." An extensive prairie along the east bank of the Kootenai River, immediately north of the mouth of Tobacco River. Tobacco was planted here by the Kutenai.

ABOVE: Stick game being played in an Upper Kootenay camp along the Kootenay River, c. 1890.

15. *Akinnu Lamqanwock*, "Snake Willows." A summer campsite located on the west side of upper Indian Creek, on land now belonging to the "69" ranch. Groups assembled here before setting out on the Summer bison hunt. Grazing was good. Prior to removal to the **Roosville-Grasmere** Reserve, the Tobacco Plains Kutenai lived here.

16. *Tco Tco Ka*. A summer site along Phillips Creek, at the International Boundary. Kootenay youths travelled long distances to seek a Supernatural helper at the rocky bluffs here

17. *Kakwaquamitu*, "Winding in and out." The early camping place of the Kootenay who hunted buffalo in the **Crowsnest Pass** region and returned across the Rockies in summer to hunt elk and plant tobacco. The term refers to the winding course of Michel Creek as it passed through a small prairie where these people camped.

18. *Kaintak,* A camp site occupied by the Michel prairie Kootenay when fishing at White Swan Lake.

19. *Akiskaqle*, "Two Ram Horns laid there." A campsite on Joseph's Prairie, a few miles east of **Cranbrook, B.C.** Game, berries and grazing for horses were available; Kootenay families long ago stayed here both summer and winter.

20. *Akam*, "Dense Woods." An important camp site located between the junction of St. Mary's river and the Kootenay, across from **Fort Steele, B.C.** Good grazing was scarce here as the region was thickly timbered.

21. *Yakikats*. A summer camping place located at **Wasa Lake.** Kootenay families often waited here for the return of buffalo hunters from the prairies.

22. *Kinvktumanke*. A prairie on the west side of the Kootenay river, south of **Skookumchuck, B.C.,** now bisected by Highway 93/95. Hunting and grazing were good here, as was the digging for certain edible roots.

23. *Akinmitukpuwat*, "Bunch Grass." A wintering site located on the east shore of **Columbia Lake**, north of **Canal Flats, B.C.** Ancient rock pictographs are nearby; Kootenay elders of the 1930's said they were made before their own forefathers' time.

24. *Yakinu Kaki*, "Rib of Yawonek." A campsite just below the **"Dutch Creek Hoodoos,"** along Highway 93/95. The great eroded rock bluff is explained in an important Kootenay legend about the monster Yawonek. Families came here to gather the abundant pine moss, which was roasted as a vegetable food in spring.

25. *Kakasi Tluk*, "Mouth of River." The main campsite at **Fairmont Hot Springs,** where Kootenay families came both for healing qualities of the waters as well as for salmon spearing in the Fall. When salmon quit running here, fishing camps moved north to the next site.

26. *Koalanuk*, "Where Lake empties into River." A popular Kootenay fishing site at **Athalmere, B.C.,** where **Windermere Lake** drains into the **Columbia River.** Fishing camps often extended uphill to where **Invermere, B.C.** is now located. Here was the site of Kootinae House, first trading post built in the region.

27. *Yakinasukwe*, "Red Water." In August, the first salmon of the season were speared at the junction of Brisco Creek with the Columbia River. In addition, the nearby hot springs were used for health benefits by all who knew of them.

28. *Yakokvki*, "Where Moss is Boiled." Now **Bonner's Ferry, Idaho,** along the Kootenay River. Families camped here in early summer to gather and roast pine moss before the start of fishing season. The site's name refers to the legendary killing of Yawonek, here.

29. *Yemoho Akamina.* A campsite southeast of **Ritz, Idaho,** where the first fishing of the season was done. Traps were set along Jack Wall slough, a short distance from the Kootenay.

30. *Hatsaxal*, "Grass." A summer base camp located just south of the International Boundary at **Porthill, Idaho** and **Kingsgate, B.C.** Fishing was done between here and a place just north of the Canadian line.

31. *Akahal.* A summer campsite in the delta region of the Kootenay, near a small lake, slightly southwest of and across from **Creston, B.C.**

32. *Kokonin.* A summer and winter campsite on the eastern edge of the delta area, along the west bank of Goat river, opposite **Creston.** There were three other major campsites in this area, all near or along the Kootenay River.

33. *Akowokinil.* A summer and winter camping place located on the west bank of the Kootenay, directly across from **Wynndel, B.C.**

BELOW: Lower Kootenay camp near Creston, B.C., c. 1895.   (CP Corp. Archives)

71

ABOVE: Lower Kootenay family by their tipi, along the Kootenay River, near Creston, B.C., c. 1900.

(B.C. Provincial Museum Photo)

Kootenay Bands

1. **Tunaxa.** A very ancient band, thought by some to have been the original Kootenay band, whose members lived practically all the time on plains and foothills of the Rocky Mountain Eastern Slopes. Their principal campground was at "The Place of Red Willow Branches," now in southwest Alberta. Epidemics and pressure from the southward-moving and more numerous Blackfeet were said to have wiped out thsi band, its survivors joining others on the west side of the mountains. Waterton River, on the east side, is called the Kootenay River in Blackfoot history and language.
2. **Tobacco Plains.** Known in the Kootenay Language as "People of the Place of the Flying Head." 1500 to 2000 Kootenays resided here in the mid-1800s; over 300 lodges into the 1880s. A sub-group of this band camped further north, at present-day Fernie, B.C., although its members frequently came back to Tobacco Plains. When the bands settled on reserves, most of the Fernie people went to the Plains, but some moved to the Columbia Lakes.
3. **Jennings.** Thought by some to have been the first large group of Kootenay to move away from the main camp at Tobacco Plains. People from the Jennings Band later scattered out to other areas. Some of them were ancestors of those now sharing a reservation with the Flatheads, around Somers, Dayton and Elmo, Montana.
4. **Libby.** A large part of the Jennings people later moved to Libby and became known as the Libby Band. In the 1850s, when peace was made between the Kutenai, Flathead and Kalispel, many people from Libby and Jennings moved to Flathead Lake and became known as "People of the Bay." This movement was led by Chief Aeneas Paul, father of the later-well-known Chief Aeneas Paul Kustata.
5. **Bonner's Ferry.** Said to have been formed when half of the Jennings-Libby people migrated further down the Kootenay River.
6. **Fort Steele.** There was a large band at this location long ago, but its members died from sickness and the survivors scattered. The present St. Mary's Band has also been the Fort Steele Band.
7. **St. Mary's.** A band which formed some time in the 1850s, largely of people from the Libby Band and some of their neighbours.
8. **Creston.** Bonner's Ferry people migrating down the Kootenay River formed the Creston Band long ago.
9. **Columbia Lake.** Led by a Chief Michel, the Columbia Lake Band was made up largely of people from Libby-Jennings who preferred to live in Canada rather than under the terms of an 1855 treaty with the United States. The Columbia Lake area is an ancient salmon fishing site for the Kootenays, so it was natural that a band should settle here.

Three Lower Kootenay Chiefs

1. Thomas (Chief "Blind") .... Leader from 1845 - 1869
2. Abraham .... 1869 - 1887
3. Maurice .... 1887 - 1900

Chiefs of the Flathead Lake Kutenai

(As recalled by Baptiste Matthias for Thain White,
Flathead Lake Lookout Museum, 1950)

1. **Feather** — Early 1700's.
2. **Going Grizzly Bear** - circa 1750, when horses were introduced to the tribe.
3. **Red Sky** — Recalled as being chief "quite a while."
4. **Michelle** — Another long-time chief, starting in the early 1800s. Led his band to settle on the shores of Flathead Lake, formerly only a seasonal campground. First white men seen in his area were two "Frenchmen" (presumably trappers) who built a cabin at Somers in 1845.

   Chief Michelle represented the Kutenais at a famous council with Governor Stevens, when he signed the "Treaty of 1855," agreeing to the Flathead Lake location as a permanent site. Ironically, Michelle later decided he liked the Columbia Lakes region in Canada better, so he left his own people and "retired" up north, in the later 1800s.
5. **Baptise** — A great warrior, elected chief after Michelle left. Was killed two years later in the area of Hungry Horse, while helping defend a Kutenai hunting camp of four lodges from a small war party of Blackfeet.
6. **Aeneas Big Knife** — Born in New York, 1828, according to a Kutenai calendar. Was chief for many years, until his death in 1900.
7. **Kustata** — Also known as Aeneas Big Knife Kustata, was son of the former chief, and himself the last "official chief" among the Flathead Lake Kutenai. Born in 1856 at Dayton, Montana, died there in 1942. This name also spelled Koostatah.

Chief Kustata in Glacier National Park, c. 1940.

Moons of the Year

Told by Stanley Como

Cold Moon
Bear Gives Birth to Young
Waters Start Running
Earth Starts Cracking
Waters Start Rising
Strawberries Ripen
Serviceberries Ripen
Berries Ripen Overnight
Wild Cherries Ripen
Leaves Are Falling
Deer Breed
Big Moon

ABOVE: Stanley Como, medicine man at St. Mary's Reserve, Cranbrook, B.C., in July, 1937. He is wearing a velvet dress shirt and beaded articles, including the top panel from a child's cradleboard, worn upside-down as a chest ornament. He was 65 at the time of this photo, and said he was born the year that a big earthquake hit the Kootenay Country. His father's father told him of the old days.

LEFT: Chiefs representing Indian people of British Columbia's Kootenay country, around 1890. Left to right, front row: Chief Abel Morning Star, Columbia Lake Band; Chief Francis Francois, St. Mary's Band; Chief Pierre Kinbasket, Shuswap Tribe; Back row: Chief Pierre Thunderbird, Government Chief of the St. Mary's Band; Chief Abel Three Feathers, Church Chief of Creston Band; Chief Alex Alexander, Government Chief of the Creston Band; Chief Francois holds his staff of office, presented by the government to all chiefs. The medal on his chest was presented in 1873 as a token of friendship between his people and the Crown. One side reads "Chief of Goodness," the other has a likeness of Queen Victoria, with her name printed beneath.

ABOVE: Chief Isadore and friends, not long after he was visited by Indian Reserve Commissioner O'Reilly. Some Kootenays hold Isadore responsible for the small amount of land contained in their reserves, claiming he "sold out" to the white men. The letter on the facing page, however, shows that the chief demanded the whole Kootenay-Columbia Valley, from the border north to Golden, B.C. It is a sad fact of British Columbia history that Indians were arbitrarily assigned to relatively small patches of their former domain by political appointees like O'Reilly, who had little knowledge of, or sympathy with, the province's original citizens. Regrettably, this attitude seems to be still common with some B.C. politicians in the 1980s.

Kneeling beside Chief Isadore, on his right, is Constable Storicum, a Colville Indian from the state of Washington, along with his young assistant. kneeling at Isadore's left, with a white hat, is Capilo, who is said to have been the cause of an "uprising" at Fort Steele in 1887. Two miners were killed near Fort Steele, after which Capilo was arrested. Chief Isadore and his men came with rifles to rescue their relative from the white man's jail. "If any of my men do wrong," said Isadore, "I am willing to have them

punished. But it is not right that, without proof, Indians should be put in prison because white men were found dead. How may Indians have been found dead, yet no white man was ever put in jail for them."

Interestingly, when Isadore brought Capilo   to court, soon after this incident, the Kootenay was acquitted. But the chief was outraged by this intrusion upon his domain, so he ordered a number of white men to leave the region. There were rumblings of further trouble between Kootenays and settlers, so the government ordered Major Sam Steele of the Mounted Police to bring 100 men and restore peace. This troop built that Fort Steele for which the area became named, although their military skills were never really needed. Their long, bungled—aboard the first home-made steamboat from Golden—took so long that the Kootenay country had already restored its own peace.

On horseback, from left to right, this picture shows: Phillip, Alpine, "Mustache Joe" (with wool cap). Skookum Joe (a noted runner), and Joseph (a chief; his father was chief when the group lived at Joseph's Prairie, or Cranbrook).

How the Kootenays were "Given" Reserves

(Excerpts from a letter written December, 1884, by
Indian Reserve Commissioner P. O'Reilly, Victoria, B.C.,
to the Superintendent-General of Indian Affairs in Ottawa)

"Sir: I have the honor to inform you that, as previously reported in my letter of the llth June, I proceeded to Kootenay (via Portland and the Northern Pacific Railroad to Sand Point), and arrived at Wild Horse Creek on the 4th July, where I was met by 'Isadore,' the Chief of the Upper Kootenay Indians, accompanied by most of his tribe.

"I explained the object of my visit, and invited them to show me what lands they most desired to have reserved. Owing, however, to their excessive demands, and not being provided with a competent interpreter, I decided to defer the consideration of their land question, and to proceed to the 'Tobacco Plains', 60 miles south . . ., where a portion of the tribe resides, 'David' being sub-chief. . .

"I found 'David' . . . quite as unreasonable in his demands as 'Isadore' had been, claiming the whole country from the boundary line to the Columbia Lakes, an area of 1,100 square miles, and I had great difficulty in inducing him to listen to any proposals to the contrary. He repeatedly referred to the large reserves allotted by the United States Government to the Indians . . . and compared them with the small area he asked for . . . and complained that Kootenay Indians had received nothing at the hands of the Dominion Government, though the Crees, Blackfeet and Stoneys, on the other side of the mountains, had been furnished with stock, seed, implements, and even rations.

". . . Having made a thorough examination of the most suitable localities, I reserved for the use of this tribe a tract of land containing 11,360 acres, consisting of open, rolling ground, interspersed with belts of timber, pine, larch and fir. The houses of this branch of the Kootenay tribe are situated in immediate proximity to the boundary line; they have four acres of land cultivated as gardens. . .

". . . On the 22nd July I returned to Wild Horse Creek, and lost no time in apprising the Indians of my readiness to confer with them. They waited upon me in a body, headed by their chief, 'Isadore.' No result was obtained, however, for several days. The chief stated, again and again, that he would not accept any limits to his reservation, unless they included the whole valley of the Kootenay and Columbia Rivers (from the International boundary line) and followed the base of the Rocky Mountains to the boat landing on the Columbia River (at Golden). He also refused to give the census of his people, the number of their stock, etc. . . .

". . . At length I decided upon the limits of reservation No. 1 . . . bounded by the St. Mary's and Kootenay Rivers . . . it contains 18,150 acres; of this some 5,000 acres are of small value, being partly wash-gravel flats on the St. Mary's River . . . the principal value of this reservation is the range to the west, containing approximately 5,000 acres of excellent bunch grass . . .

"On this reserve . . . about sixteen acres were cultivated without irrigation; the soil is poor and gravelly, and crops are consequently light. The principal village . . . of forty-seven houses is situated on the south bank of the St. Mary's River, on the property of the Rev. Father Fouquet. The 'St. Eugene Mission' has been established by the Roman Catholics . . . and here the Indians congregate during the winter months.

"On the 5th of August I arrived at the Lower Columbia Lake (Lake Windermere), the place of residence of another portion of the Kootenay tribe, and of whom 'Moyeas' is the chief. Here, again, I was met by requests for a greater area of land than I considered necessary, although their demands were not so excessive ... and I found them more amenable to reason. They also had a greater claim to favourable consideration, as they had evidently done their best to fence and cultivate such portions of the land as could be irrigated, and had erected comfortable houses for themselves, which they showed me with commendable pride ... I decided to allot them ... 8,320 acres...

"On completing my work in the Upper Kootenay Valley, I proceeded to visit that of the Lower Kootenay ... on the 26th of August ...

"... The Indians asked that land be given them on the right bank of the Kootenay River, about 2½ miles north of the International boundary line., I acceded to their request, and made Reservation No. 4, though most reluctantly, for a more worthless piece of land, in its present condition, cannot well be imagined.

"Of the 1,600 acres so reserved, 1,200 are swampy marsh land ... Should the Kootenay reclamation scheme be carried out, the whole ... could be brought into cultivation...

"This branch of the Kootenay tribe is the least advanced in civilization, being far removed from any white settlement. Formerly, they crossed the Rocky Mountains to hunt, but the buffalo being exterminated, they now depend principally on fish and berries ... They number fifty-two men, thirty-five women and seventy-three children, a total of 160, of whom 'St. Pierre' is the sub-chief.

"In conclusion, I think it well to state again, that I have experienced very great difficulty in dealing with the Indians of the Kootenay country ... But I am glad to say that finally they appeared satisfied with the allotments made for them, and which, I believe, will not materially interfere with white settlement."

BELOW: St. Eugene Mission and homes of the St. Mary's Reserve, c. 1895.

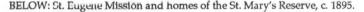

Joseph's Prairie Turns into Cranbrook, and the Kootenays Move On

Recalled by Barnaby, of the St. Mary's Reserve, in 1937.

"My people camped in the area now called Cranbrook, B.C., long before any settlers and miners arrived. We call this place *Kai-ya-kawana-sukpu*, which means 'Pine Tree in the Centre.' The settlers who first came called it Joseph's Prairie, because the chief of our band was named Joseph.

"Joseph was the first chief of our band, the *Akamnik*, formed in my father's time from three other bands, at Libby, Tobacco Plains and Bonner's Ferry. People from these groups joined together under Joseph, who led them to the Columbia Lakes for salmon fishing. When that finished they moved down to the Cranbrook area and made that their winter camp, or band headquarters.

"The actual camping spot was a little east from where the town was built, a place that had good water and grazing, plus a lot of wild berries. We called this place 'Two Ram Horns Laid There,' which had something to do with mountain sheep, which were hunted in mountains nearby. Long before our band came into existence, this was the base camp for another large Kootenay band that was wiped out from some sickness before my father's time.

ABOVE: Barnaby, Kootenay medecine man and member of the Akamnik Band, seen by his home on the St. Mary's Reserve, outside Cranbrook, B.C., in 1937.

LEFT: A Kootenay mother and daughter on their well-maintained ranch near Cranbrook, around 1900. Some bands got small herds of livestock soon after buffalo disappeared from the plains, in the early 1880s. Kootenay farming was carried on for many years as a cooperative effort within the various bands.

"When settlers started moving into Joseph's Prairie our people didn't like it. There were about 150 of us, and soon there were more of them. Their cattle and horses used up the grazing, and there was some trouble with liquor, so the chief decided we should move on. We had other places up and down the valley that we camped at, but none were as well-liked as Cranbrook. We *gave* Cranbrook to British Columbia! When will they thank us for it?

"We moved to the junction of the St. Mary's and Kootenay Rivers, down along the forest and river bottoms from where Fort Steele now sits. It is for this place that our band was named Akamnik, 'people of the thick woods.' If we had stayed there we might have become known as the 'Fort Steele Kootenay,' instead of the St. Mary's Band. But around the time I was a small boy (in the year 1874), Catholic priests and nuns built St. Eugene's Mission, up the St. Mary's River a few miles, so we all moved there, and that is where the government made our reserve.

"It was a big mistake for us to move in by the missionaries, because they only confused our people, and forced them to give up their old ways and beliefs. We should have stayed by ourselves and had a large reserve with the other Kootenays, then we would still be practicing our natural life."

Kutenai Sun Dance

Told By Baptiste Matthias,
Kutenai Sun Dance Leader at Elmo, Montana, in 1937.

We Kutenais were the only ones living on the west side of the Rocky Mountains to practice a Sun Dance. It was given to our ancestors long ago, when they still lived over on the prairies a lot of the time. The way we perform this ceremony is different from other tribes. We all do it the way we learned it.

"It all comes from visions and dreams; that's how the spirits give us directions. I had two uncles who were leaders of Sun Dances, so I must have learned from them. The spirits speak to us in mysterious ways, and I learned this while still young.

"I have put up four Sun Dances so far in my life (he put up three more afterwards, the last one near Flathead Lake in 1947). It is a big sacrifice for me, but I do this for my people. I would like to make more Sun Dances, but it is getting harder all the time. I need many people to help me with the ceremony, and those who know about it are dying off rapidly. The missionaries have discouraged our younger people from learning about these things, although they are just as good as the things we do in church.

"The last big Kutenai Sun Dance I can remember was just before the year 1900, at Tobacco Plains. Just about every Kutenai was there, no matter from what band. We camped in a big circle of tipis that spread far out over the plain. I suppose I will never see such a camp of Kutenais again. We had a Sun Dance at Tobacco Plains about five years ago, but the circle was not even one-quarter the size.

"The Sun Dance is a ceremony to honor the Sun, and also to give thanks for all other forms of Life. In former times, every Kutenai person attended the Sun Dance ceremony, which was held each and every year. It was the center of our tribal life, and the Sun Lodge was the center of our Universe."

LEFT: Kutenai Sun Dance leader Baptiste Matthias, at Dayton, Montana in July 1937. he is wearing his ceremonial buckskin shirt, the sign of his sacred office, along with the belt made of otter fur. The claw and shell necklace was his personal power symbol. He was respected as a kind man, wise as a ceremonial leader and tribal storyteller, with skills for craftwork such as pipe makeing.
RIGHT: Mrs. Baptiste Matthias, in the meadow by their home in Elmo, Montana in 1937.

ABOVE: The last Sun Dances held by the Kutenais were near Flathead Lake during the 1940's. In this scene the sacred Sun Lodge is being raised, while the Sun Dance leader's assistant stands up in the symbolic "eagle's nest," surveying the Kutenai country for the blessings of nature. At the final Sun Dance, led by Baptiste Matthias in 1947, Basso Jocko was the individual who stood up on the lodge when it was raised. He also fulfilled the special duties of locating the main pole and ritually preparing it, both functions he learned as a young man from his elders.

A vital part of the Sun Dance ceremony was the preparation of a doll, or effigy, which represented the Creator of the Universe, and symbolic of the many prayers made by the leader and his people. Joe Antiste produced the final doll, while Anna Marie Paul made its special miniature clothing. The Sun Dance cerermonies ended with the taking of these special dolls far out into the wilds, where they were left for the spiritual benefit of all Kutenai people.

Anyone in the tribe could dance and receive blessigns from the ceremony, but certain participants were called Whistlers, and their duties required further training. In 1947 Modiste Eneas and Basile Left Hand were the two Whistlers, while Peter Paul was their instructor, or "driver."

Madeline Left Hand was in charge of the ceremonial deer hoof rattles - some mounted on a staff, others tied together with thongs into a bunch. She performed this role all her life, but no one took over the role upon her death. Nine or ten drummers provided the final ceremony's background music.

Some Chiefs of the St. Mary's Band

1. Joseph - 1870s and '80s.
2. Francois - 1894 - 1923.
3. Adrian - 1923 - 1933.
4. Eusta - 1933 -
5. Aloysius Birdstone - 1953
6. Joseph Whitehead - 1957 - 1963.
7. Aloysius Birdstone - 1965.

Some Chiefs of the Tobacco Plains Band

1. Edward David - 1871 - 1891.
2. Paul David - 1891 - 1946
3. Pierre Shottanana - 1946 - 1952.
4. Augustine Ignatius - 1952 - 1954.
5. Nicholas Gravelle - 1954 - 1960.
6. Elizabeth Gravelle - 1960 - 1962.
7. Ambrose Gravelle - 1964 - 1968.

1979 Upper Kootenay Census

St. Mary's Band - 218
Tobacco Plains - 93
Columbia Lake - 183

Three Basic Principles Taught to Kootenay Boys by Their Fathers and Uncles

1. "Do not let anyone hear you but the family you are visiting, lest the old women ridicule you."
2. "Try and get up before anyone else. Take your bow and hunt. True, the girls will not see your face because you are out hunting every day, but they will know your fame and will want to marry you. That is surer and better than strutting around before them all the time."
3. "One cannot keep a lie, and when the truth is known the camp will be told and its laughter will make you ashamed."

85

ABOVE: Kootenay leaders and a missionary priest at Lake Windermere, B.C. about 1932. From left to right: Chief Paul David; priest; chief Francis Francois and wife Spider; Louie Arbell and wife; Pierre Cronin, also known as Moneyhead, who staked a claim on a successful mine at Moyie, B.C. that made him the richest Kootenay Indian of his time. His money helped build the St. Mary's mission church, still standing near Cranbrook, B.C. The man behind him with a hat is not known.

(Topical Press Agency Photo)

BONNER'S FERRY KUTENAI

Most U.S. Kutenais live along Flathead Lake, on a reservation shared with the Flathead-Salish. One small group lives on 2,695 acres of allotted land by Bonner's Ferry, Idaho, where their forefathers camped. In 1969, this group had 67 enrolled members, of whom 60 lived on the reservation. In 1980 the number of residents was down to 40. The band operates a high quality motor hotel, restaurant and gift shop, known as the "Kootenai River Inn."

Bibliography

Boas, F., *Kutenai Tales*, Bulletin 59. Bureau of American Ethnology, Washington, 1918.

Chamberlain, A.F., *The Kootenay Indians*. Annual Archeological Report, Toronto, 1906.

Schaeffer, Claude E., *Unpublished Field Notes among the Kutenai*, 1930's to 1960's. American Meseum of Natural History, New York, and Glenbow-Alberta Institute Archives, Calgary.

Turney-High, H.H. *Ethnography of the Kutenai*. Memoirs of the American Anthropological Association No. 56, Menasha, Wisconsin, 1941.

White, Thain, Flathead Lake Lookout Museum Papers. Lakeside, Montana, 1950's.

ABOVE: A typical home in the early years of the Flathead Reservation. Most families built log cabins, but used tipis when the weather was good.

Flathead Origins

"I was told that it was a mistake by the white people, calling the Indians the Flatheads," said a tribal elder named Pierre Adams, many years ago. "The reason why they were called Flatheads, there were people from around Umatilla, Oregon, who had the custom of flattening their children's heads by strapping them on a board. These people were visiting the Salish in this part of the country and some of the whites thought they belonged here and called us Flatheads."

Elders like Pierre recalled migration legends that told how their forefathers came to the Rocky Mountains from the west, where they lived near Indians with flat heads. Most Salish-speaking Indians still do live near the Pacific coast.

They say there was once a big fight in which Salish relatives and friends killed each other. The fight was over something foolish: two leaders argued about whether flying ducks quack with their bills or their wings. They finally called a truce to the fighting, but one of the leaders set out with his followers to seek a new homeland. They ended up in the beautiful Bitterroot Valley of Western Montana, a place considered to be *the* traditional Flathead-Salish home.

Another Salish-speaking group, the Pend d'Oreilles, were already using the Bitterroot Valley for a camping site, but in a show of friendship they agreed to let the Flatheads settle there, while they moved to another of their favorite areas, further North. In later times some of the Flathead people moved closer to the Pend d'Oreilles, especially after Catholic priests built St. Ignatius mission, in a valley about mid-way between the two groups.

There were others who lived in the mountains and valleys before the Flatheads came, and for a time after their arrival, although stories about these beings are as much mystery as history. In addition to dwarfs and giants, there were crude, dumb, primitive people called the "Foolish Folk." It is said these people slowly died out because of their foolishness, the last big group going all at once, following an especially-foolish chief over Spokane Falls in their canoes! None survived this chief's efforts to "show off."

ABOVE: Western Montana's Jocko Valley forms the southern end of the Flathead Reservation. This c. 1930 scene shows the big 4th of July celebration held by the tribe each year in Arlee. The race track is on the left, tipi camp and pow-wow arena on the right.

Flathead Country

The Flathead Reservation of today is in a beautiful part of western Montana, along the foothills of the Rocky Mountains. It runs from Flathead Lake south, almost to the city of Missoula. On the West is the majestic Bitterroot range of mountains. This reservation is shared with a division of the Kutenai tribe, whose members live around Flathead Lake.

The old-time Flathead country included much of what is now western Montana. Home base was the Bitterroot Valley, a larger version of the similar valley in which the people live, today. Back when buffalo herds roamed the Plains, across the Rocky Mountains, the Flathead people spent much of their time camping and hunting on that side. In fact, they probably spent most of their time on the Prairies until the Southward moving Blackfoot people arrived in the early 1800s. They were more aggressive and much more numerous, so that the Flatheads were forced to seek more secluded areas for their permanent campgrounds. It is assumed that the Bitterroot Valley was then chosen as a permanent home. After that time, camping on the open plains became limited to excursions for buffalo hunting. The hunting parties travelled as light as possible and well-armed in case of attack. Often the Flatheads were joined by hunters from many of the tribes further West, who wanted buffalo hides, but were afraid to go after them alone. Most of this buffalo hunting was done in the area around Great Falls, Helena, and Butte, Montana.

By tradition, the main buffalo hunt was a great tribal affair that lasted all Fall. Old people and mothers with many children were usually left in secluded camps back in the Bitterroot Valley. A small group of younger men stayed behind to protect them and help care for the extra horses and equipment that the main group did not wish to haul out on the plains. Just before the heavy snows of Winter set in, the main group would return with a fresh supply of warm buffalo robes and dried buffalo meat. Sometimes the snows came too early and the hunting people were forced to winter on the East side of the mountains.

The Flathead people did not travel West far beyond the summit of the Bitterroot Mountains. They followed an ancient trail along Lolo Creek, through Lolo Pass, to reach the Westward-flowing waters where they could catch salmon. Because there were no salmon on their side of the mountains, the old people called Lolo Creek "No Salmon River."

A few miles below the place where Lolo Creek joins the Bitterroot River was the most important camping place in the valley. It was called "Large Space of Open Prairie," located about four miles North of the present town of Stevensville. That place had plenty of grazing for horses, as well as good supplies of Camas roots and wild berries.

The area round the city of Missoula was popular for camping because plenty of grazing was available there. North of the city was "Where the River Trees End," and a place called "Tree Whose Limbs are Stripped off." East of the city was a place called "Katalsa," where Camas grew in quantity. The Missoula River is said to have been called "Shining Waters," as the result of a legend in which Coyote was lured to the area by beautiful dancing girls who made the waters shine.

Even in the "Old Days" the people regularly went North to the valley of the Jocko River, where they live today. A popular campsite there was called "Little Draw." The Jocko River was called "Creek of the Wild Plum Trees," after a legend in which Coyote threw down his whip and watched a plum tree grow up from it.

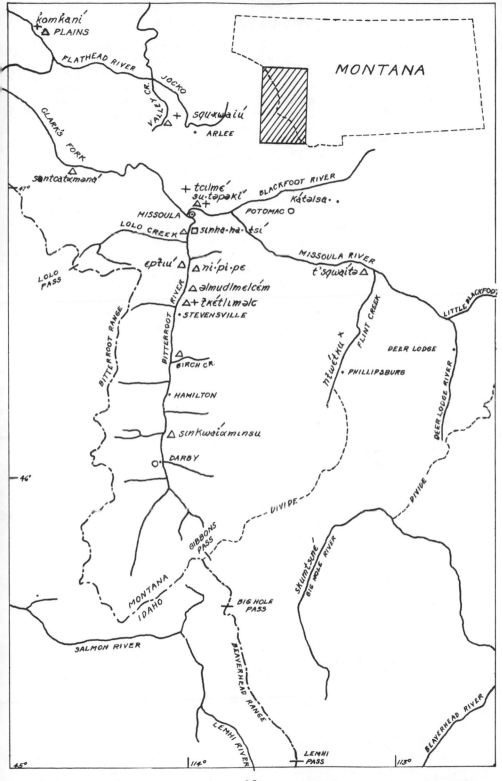

komkani'
+
△ PLAINS

FLATHEAD RIVER

JOCKO

VALLEY CR.

CLARK'S FORK

MONTANA

squ·kwaiú'
+
△
• ARLEE

santcatᴇmᴇnᴇ'
△

+ tcᴜlme'
su·tᴇpᴇki'
+ △

BLACKFOOT RIVER

kátᴇlsᴇ· .

MISSOULA ◎
LOLO CREEK △

POTOMAC ○

□ sᴜnhᴇ·hᴇ·tsi'

LOLO PASS

epᵗɪu' △

△ ni·pi·pe

MISSOULA RIVER

t'sqwaitᴇ △

BITTERROOT RIVER

△ ᴇlmᴜdᴌmᴇlcém

BITTERROOT RANGE

△ + ᴌkétᴌɪmᴇlc
• STEVENSVILLE

nᴌwétku ×

FLINT CREEK

LITTLE BLACKFOOT

△
BIRCH CR.

DEER LODGE

• HAMILTON

• PHILLIPSBURG

DEER LODGE RIVER

△ sᴜnkwaiᴇmᴜnsu

○ DARBY

DIVIDE

DIVIDE

GIBBONS PASS

skum-tsuné -

BIG HOLE RIVER

MONTANA
IDAHO

BIG HOLE PASS

SALMON RIVER

BEAVERHEAD RANGE

BEAVERHEAD RIVER

LEMHI RIVER

LEMHI PASS

47°

46°

45°

114°

113°

90

The Welcoming of Strangers

In a region where native tribes were feared for their cunning and aggressiveness, the Flathead people stood out like an island of safety and friendship. Even critical missionaries of the last century credited the Flatheads with having the virtues of modesty, frankness, courage, goodness and generosity. "A nation of chiefs," said one of the Catholic priests. Although the people bravely fought their hereditary enemies — Blackfoot, Shoshone, Gros Ventre and Sioux — they never once fought against the Westward moving white men, who later cheated the tribe out of the Bitterroot Valley.

An important result of Flathead friendliness was the early intermarriage with people from other tribes and other countries. According to Father Ravalli — a Catholic priest who spent most of his life among the Flatheads and who probably recorded histories of all the families in the course of his well-accepted baptisms — there were no pure-blood Flatheads in the tribe in 1875. In the 1920s the ethnographer Teit was given a list of the tribes with whom the Flathead had intermarried. Included were: Kutenai, Blackfoot, Shoshone, Nez Perce, Crow, Pend d'Oreille, Kalispel, Spokan, Coeur d'Alene, Colville, Sanpoil, Okanagan, Columbia, Shuswap, Thompson, Lillooet, Cherokee, Chippewa, Delaware, Shawnee and Iroquois.

A notorious case of intermarriage was recorded by Teit. A man named John Grant lived among the people. His mother was from the nearby Kalispel tribe; his father had been a trader for the Hudson's Bay Company. Grant lived in a round house with six bedrooms, each occupied by one of his six wives. Each wife was from a different tribe, including Crow and Shoshone. He later left his wives and children and took off to Red River, Manitoba. His descendants stayed on the reservation and intermarried there.

It is interesting to hear of people from the Delaware, Shawnee and Iroquois tribes living among the Flatheads. Those tribes are from the East of the continent, a long ways from Flathead country. They first came out West around 1800, as employees of traders and trappers. When they returned East they must have given glowing accounts of Flathead friendliness along with descriptions of the beautiful, wild country in which the native people lived, almost undisturbed. By that time, tribes in the East had already suffered long at the hands of invaders from across the oceans.

One Iroquois who returned East with good thoughts of the Flatheads was Ignace La Mousse — also known as Old Ignace. He formed a party of 24 emigrants from among his people of the East. Sometime around 1815 the party left their homeland, around Montreal, Quebec, and joined the Flathead tribe. Thus, many Flatheads have distant relatives in French-speaking Canada.

Some of the Iroquois in Old Ignace's party had white ancestors, whose traits were soon passed to the Flatheads. An equally-important contribution was made to Flathead life by these Iroquois with the introduction of the Catholic religion. The Flatheads were inspired by what they had learned of Catholicism, and decided they wanted to know more. Accordingly, a mixed group of Flatheads and interested Nez Perces headed for Catholic headquarters in far-away St. Louis.

This first Flathead party did not succeed in returning with a Catholic priest, as they had hoped to do. Of those who left, only one made it all the way to St. Louis and back. A few years later, in 1835, a second delegation set out for St. Louis — this time led by Ignace La Mousse. Still no Catholic priests came back with them. A third delegation joined a large party of other natives who were being led East by a missionary. This party was wiped out by Sioux, along the way. A fourth delegation was also led by Ignace.

This one finally succeeded in persuading the famous Father De Smet to come out and visit the Flatheads in 1840.

In 1841 De Smet came back to the Flatheads and brought along five assistants. With the help of the people they soon built St. Mary's mission in the midst of the Bitterroot Valley. But after all their efforts to learn about the Catholic religion, the Flatheads were soon discouraged by the attitudes of the priests. The people had wanted to *add* Catholicism to their own Ways of Life — not to exchange *their* ways for the ways that the priests demanded. In 1850 the mission was forced to close. It did not reopen until 1866, although the people continued on their own with the teachings they had already learned.

BELOW: In a Missoula Studio, c. 1890.

The Emigration of Jim Delaware

One of the people who came from the East to join the Flathead tribe was Jim Delaware, whose son, John, died just a few years back. Jim was a young Delaware named "Tree-with-a-dry-top" when he pursuaded his father to let him join a small trapping party that was headed West. His father gave him two horses and the necessary equipment.

He left his country in the East with six other men. They began their journey in the Springtime and were soon joined by three white men also headed West. They were all captured by a Sioux war party, who kept the white men as prisoners but let the Delawares go.

Further West the party was attacked by a group of Shoshone who took most of their horses. The Delawares also had a mule, which one of the enemy tried to mount. It kicked him off, and the man was killed by the father of John Hill (who later was a flathead delegate to Washington, D.C. in 1887, while the government was trying to remove the tribe from Bitterroot Valley). At least one other enemy was killed before the encounter was over.

The Deleware party exchanged their furs at trading posts along the way, until they reached California. There, they spent Winter along the Pacific Ocean, meeting with other native people, as well as whites and Mexicans.

The following Spring the party left California and headed North and East. They passed through a great desert where several of their horses died. At one point they were so thirsty they drank the blood of a lone buffalo bull that they found. They continued to trap along the way. They again encountered the Shoshone, but this time on peaceful terms. Three of the party stayed for a year or two with the Shoshone, while the rest went on. Those who stayed included John Delaware's father, John Hill's father, and a Shawnee man named Shawnee Jake. All of them ended up among the Flatheads. Shawnee Jake married a Shoshone woman and left her with a son, before he moved on.

While Shawnee Jake remained with the Shoshone for a longer time, the other two men moved on the following Spring. By Winter they had joined the Nez Perce People and married two of their women. Jim Deleware left a daughter when he finally moved on from the Nez Perce. John Hill was born as a result of the marriage of his father and a Nez Perce woman.

Jim Deleware finally decided to return to his home in the East, by himself. He left the Nez Perce and travelled until he came to the Bitterroot Valley. There he met a Shawnee man named Ben Kaiser, who was ill. Jim was pursuaded to stay and look after Kaiser. By the time the latter became well enough to marry a Flathead woman, Jim Deleware had already found himself a Flathead wife.

The last names of these different men from Eastern tribes are among some of the most common ones today on the Flathead reservation. Not only did these emigrants add their physical heritage to the Flatheads, they also added some of their knowledge of life. The Flatheads learned to build log cabins at their Winter camps in the Bitterroot Valley, and they were eager to obtain seeds from the Catholic missionaries after the men from the East told them about cultivating such crops as Corn and grains.

. . . Said an old Flathead man to the Catholic missionary who asked him if he ever prayed before the arrival of the priests: "Oh yes, every morning my mother took me into the woods, and having found a dry pine-tree, broken and rotten from old age, she told me, 'My son, go and rub yourself against that tree and pray.' And so I did, saying: 'Oh good tree! have pity on me and let me live as long as you lived'."

ABOVE: John Delaware, son of a Flathead woman and a Delaware man, himself a highly-respected elder on the Flathead Reservation, 1934.

Treaty Making

"Before the Black Robes (Catholic priests) came and we lived in this valley (Bitter-root), each year we used to choose a boy and send him to the top of the mountain," said old Moise in later years, "and he fasted there and made Medicine for the people. The he came back and we were well. That was all the studying we had to do then . . . .The valley was our home. If we had not learned to think, we would not have been driven out."

As you may tell from that statement, the treaty-making chapter in Flathead history is no more cheerful that that of any other tribe, unless you're a politician, or a land-hungry pioneer who sees all land for its economic potential rather that its spiritual value to nature.

The U.S. Government chose the year 1855 as one in which to place the Flathead people and their neighbours under government 'law and order'. Of course the native people knew nothing about this, so they willingly signed treaty papers that were presented to them. After all, the government agent was welcomed as a 'friend among friends'. Even *if* the people *had* known what the Treaty papers *really* meant, they could not have denied granting a guest's wish. *All* he asked them to do was *sign* some papers about *distant* parts of their country that they would give up to others who wanted them more.

The agent, a Governor Stevens of Washington Territory, was able to get all the chiefs to sign over to the government an area of some 23,000 square miles. In exchange he 'gave' them a reservation of about 2,000 square miles, complete with "doctor, blacksmith, farmer, wheelwright, teacher, and their respective institutions". The Indian people thought they were to settle in their favourite old-time lands, and they were eager to learn how to make their settled lives more successful — like those of white farmers.

Hot weather during the days of the 1855 Treaty Council may have caused everyone to seek a hurried conclusion. At any rate, when Flathead Head Chief, Victor (father of Charlo), took too long to make up his mind about where he wanted to settle his people, the noble Governor called him "an old woman and a dog!". The chief withdrew from the council because of the insult, so the Governor noted in his diary, "Victor is now thinking and studying over this matter." Indeed, he was! He refused the Gover-nor's one last wish — to move his people out of the Bitterroot Valley to an area further North.

For seventeen years following the council with Governor Stevens, the Flatheads lived their usual lives in the Bitterroot Valley. White settlers moved into the valley and built up farms, but there seemed to be enough land for everyone, and peace certainly did prevail. No government inspection of the valley was made — though promised by the treaty — and no doctors or teachers ever came. The whole treaty had been pretty much forgotten, in fact. Most of is signers had died, and Victor's son, Charlo, had inherited leadership of the tribe.

Flatheads were still making regular trips to the Prairies for buffalo hunting. In addi-tion, they had log cabins in the Bitterroot Valley. Their horse herds were large and healthy, and they bought cattle from emigrants coming West. These rapidly increased, providing milk and meat. Families grew their own grain and garden crops. Until too many white farmers moved in and broke up the land, horses had been able to share the abundant wild pastures with wild animals.

But the continuing flow of white settlers into the Bitterroot Valley drew the government's attention to a problem: Flatheads were taking up too much of the Valley's choice land, and conflicts were brewing.

Accordingly, the U.S. government hatched a scheme, sending General Garfield to the Bitterroot Valley to carry it out. Garfield went to the Flathead people in 1872 with an order which claimed the government had "carefully surveyed and examined" the Bitterroot Valley and had decided that "all Indians residing in said Bitterroot Valley be removed as soon as practicable." As incentive for moving, they were to be given log houses, a year's supply of wheat, and "such potatoes and other vegetables as can be spared from the agency farm, a number of agricultural implements, and $50,000 to be paid in ten annual installments." The agreement was signed by General Garfield, Head Chief Charlo, and minor chiefs Arlee and Adolf.

People were amazed when they saw the published agreement, especially with Charlo's signature. None was quite so amazed, however, as Charlo himself! He *insisted* that he never signed the agreement. Later, the original document was inspected in Washington. Charlo's signature was not on it! Confronted with this evidence, General Garfield claimed he had reported the document signed because he thought Charlo would agree and sign it, once he saw that his people were actually being moved. He had been told that unless he signed, his people would not be given the promised benefits.

So, Arlee and Adolf led *some* Flatheads to the new reservation to join others who had moved there before. Arlee was then appointed head chief of the Flatheads by the government, and given $50,000 for his followers, plus a salary for himself, for the "sale of the Bitterroot Valley." Charlo and most of his people stayed in the Bitterroots and got nothing.

More years passed before the visit of another government delegation, in 1883. This resulted in a trip to Washington, D.C. by Charlo and his head men in 1884. With him went Antoine Moise (Crane with a Ring around his Neck), Louis Vanderburg (Grizzly Bear far Away), John Hill (Hand Shot Off), and Abel (Red Arm). For nearly a month the leaders heard government attempts to persuade their move out of the Bitterroot Valley. Charlo agreed to nothing except that his people were free to move, if they desired. As for himself, he only wished to live and die in the valley that his ancestors had called home.

When the delegation returned from Washington, twenty-one families decided to move North and take up residence on the government reservation. This left about 350 people to live under Charlo's leadership. One by one, other families left their beloved valley as the years went by. Buffalo were gone from the plains, and so went a major source of food and warmth. The new settlers used up much of the old hunting and gathering land. And, without much outside help, the people's attempts at farming were not successful enough to support the tribe. Bootleggers and unscrupulous settlers sold liquor to those Flatheads who wanted it and could pay.

Finally in 1891 the government sent General Carrington to see Charlo, in an effort to persuade him to move. Major Ronan, the reservation agent and an acquaintance of Charlo's, took part in the discussion. Finally, Charo told the government men: "I will go — I and my children. My young men are becoming bad; they have no place to hunt. I do not want the land you promise. I do not believe your promises. All I want is enough ground for my grave. We will go over there."

It was a cool morning in the Fall of 1891, when the last group of Flatheads packed up their camps and belongings to ride away from the Bitterroot Valley. Charo and his head-men led them North. One more night they camped along the Bitterroot River, then they passed Missoula and camped northwest of there, at the foot of the pass which led into the reservation. The next day the people were welcomed by their relatives, who helped them set up their camps around the Jocko River. Here they have lived ever since. But always those who had been "Charlo's People" spoke of the Bitterroot Valley with hushed and sad tones of reverence—like a beloved mother, passed away.

For more than one hundred years the Flathead people were led by head chiefs from the same family—each passed duties of his office on to one of his sons. Beginning with Victor, in 1854, this family reign ended with the death of his great-grandson, Paul Charlo, in 1957.

Flathead people were extremely loyal to their head chiefs, who kept their positions for as long as they lived. The Flathead name for the head chief was "Ilimigum," which translates as 'Master'. He spoke of the people as his "children" and devoted his life to them accordingly.

In the old days the people raised their children to have respect and to give complete obedience to the head chief. Although the head chief always had a council of minor chiefs with whom he discussed tribal matters, his own decisions and orders were accepted and followed by everyone.

Because the head chief held so much power over his people he was always expected to be a distinguished man, known for honesty, wisdom, generosity and courage. He and his family were expected to live without signs of jealousy, anger or fear. Those of his people who disobeyed tribal rules were brought before him to receive stern lectures and discipline, including severe whippings. One of the head chief's badges of office—which he carried with him most of the time—was an official whip. The other badge of office was the tribal pipe—one that was smoked before any important discussion or meeting took place involving tribal matters.

The earliest chief known to Flathead history was named *Big Hawk*. He was killed in the late 1700's while out in buffalo country around the Missouri River. He was succeeded by Tceleskaimi, or *Three Eagles*, who is thought to have been the son of Big Hawk. Three Eagles was leader of the Flathead people when they met the Lewis and Clark party, in 1805, and saw their first white and black men. They thought the black man was a white man whose face was painted black in preparation for a scalp dance.

Three Eagles was succeeded by *Standing Grizzly Bear*, also known as *Loyolo* after the priests arrived and gave such names to the people. Loyolo died in 1854 without choosing a successor. *Plenty-of-Horses*, or *Victor*, was then elected to become head chief. Victor was born in 1790, and died during a summer buffalo hunt in 1870. Historians have a record of his abilities as a good leader from the diaries of the 1855 Treaty.

When Victor died in 1870, his son, *Charlo*, became head chief. Charlo's other name was *Small Grizzly Bear Claw*, but the people usually just called him Charlo. He was born around 1830, and he died around 1910 at the age of 80. In his young days Charlo was a fearless warrior and hunter. He later named one of his dogs "Sharp Cry," in memory of an enemy who had made such a sound just before Charlo stabbed him to death.

Charlo's son, *Martin*, used to talk about the successful farm that the Charlo family had while they were living their old life in the Bitterroot Valley. The head chief always tried to set a good example for his people. He kept cattle and horses, grew vegetables and grain, and went to the mission church regularly. He had over sixty horses in his herd. Many of them he loaned out to members of his tribe who were less fortunate or ambitious.

BELOW: Chief Charlot, or Bear Claw (sitting), with Pascal Antoine, or Bear Blood (standing) in Washington, D.C., February, 1905. (DeLaney Gill Photo, Smithsonian Institution)

One time the Flathead people were returning from a Buffalo hunt on the Prairies when they were attacked by enemies. Charlo's father-in-law was killed, and most of the family's horses were captured. The Flathead party consisted of ten lodges, whose covers were afterwards packed on two oxen that Charlo had obtained from a white settler. This was in the area of Deer Lodge, Montana. His son, Martin, rode back to the Bitterroot Valley on a yearling colt.

While he still lived in the Bitterroot Valley, Chief Charlo not only welcomed white settlers to live by his people, he even risked his life to protect them. When Chief Joseph led his Nez Perce people on their famous retreat towards Canada, he sent word to his old friend, Charlo, that he needed help and supplies. White settlers and their government had driven the Nez Perce from their ancestral valley just as they were then trying to drive out the Flatheads. Joseph thought their common predicaments might unite Charlo's people with his own.

Instead of helping Joseph, however, Charlo sent word back that his old friend should stay clear of the Flathead country and cause no harm to any settlers within it. Otherwise, he warned, Flathead warriors would have to be sent out to defend the settlers from the Nez Perce. The same settlers, and their government, later forged Charlo's signature and took away his lands.

Charlo spent the last twenty years of his life serving his people while mourning the loss of their old country and the ways of life that went with it. He made regular visits to the homes of his followers, going on horseback, and he attended all the tribe's ceremonies and dances. However, he seldom trusted outsiders and had little to do with them. He wore a look of sadness wherever he went.

Martin Charlo followed his father as head chief of the Flathead-Salish. Born in 1865, Martin knew the old ways of life, and also mourned the loss of their Valley. Nevertheless, he worked hard to make his people combine peacefulness and honesty with benefits available from agriculture and social cooperation on the reservation. Flathead farms were as well-equipped and thriving as many farms off the reservation. It was common to see horse-drawn plows, buggies, and hay wagons being operated by men with long braids and buckskin moccasins.

In 1935, during the time of Martin Charlo, the Reorganization Act was drawn up by the government and handed to the tribes. The Act was welcomed by progressive people because it provided the tribes with constitutions, by-laws, and elected councilmen—ten of them, on the Flathead reservation. The Act made no provision for a head chief after the death of Martin Charlo, although tradition-oriented members of the tribe elected Martin's son, Paul Charlo.

The Tribal Council went along with this election to the extent of making Paul Charlo their 'honorary chief'. His followers treated him with the traditional respect and loyalty given to a head chief, although he had no legal powers within the tribe. He represented his people at Washington, D.C. in 1953, when the government tried to pass a bill terminating reservations. Until his death in 1957 he always kept up with government and tribal council activities, speaking up whenever he felt the rights of his people threatened. He was particularly opposed to the many efforts that were made to sell, steal, or give away remaining Flathead lands.

ABOVE: Flathead chiefs meeting with government delegation in 1907. From left to right: Louison, or Red Owl, a minor chief and tribal judge; Joe La Mousse, a minor chief and great warrior; Antoine Moise, the same; Three Heads, a medicine man; Chief Charlot; his son, Martin Charlo; Big Sam, a great warrior and the Chief's announcer.
(Edward H. Boos Photo, Missoula)

Chief Antoine Moise

One of Charlo's minor chiefs at the time when he led the people away from the Bitterroot Valley was *Antoine Moise*, also known as Door-of-the-Grizzly-Bear-Lodge. The name Moise is said to be a variation of Mousse. Moise was an ancestor of the Iroquois, Ignace La Mousse.

Moise was one of the most famous and daring warriors among the Flatheads, in the Old Days. The ethnographer Teit made this comment in the 1920's: "At the Fourth of July dances on the reserve I saw Chief Moise recount his experiences in battles with the Blackfeet and Crow. He appeared wearing only moccasins, breechclout, necklace, armlets, and headband. His whole body was painted yellow except the right leg below the calf, which was painted red. He explained that he was painted this way because the deeds he narrated took place on the Yellowstone in a great battle with the Blackfoot. He held in one hand a ceremonial weapon like a spear, the blade of which he stuck into the ground. It had a large iron head and was wrapped with otter skin from the blade to the end. The butt end was bent over and formed a loop. This ceremonial weapon was a token of his bravery. Only a man who had advanced in battle to within touching distance of the enemy in the face of superior numbers was entitled to carry this kind of spear at the dances and parades."

During the last years in the Bitterroot Valley, Antoine Moise was involved in a drunken party during which he killed a man in self defense. He immediately went to Charlo, as was the custom, and admitted the killing. He was accompanied by several of his relatives to protect him in case the killed man's family should seek revenge before the head chief could settle the matter. Charlo was mourning, at that time, over the loss of one of his children. Many people were gathered at his home for that reason.

When Charlo learned the purpose of Moise's visit, he told Moise to take of his clothes and to lie on the floor. The chief then lectured Moise, while everyone watched. After the lecture he took up his whip and began lashing Moise up the back, starting at the buttocks. With each stroke of the whip the Chief said one 'Hail Mary'. Over three rosaries were said, and over 200 strokes from the whip were administered, before the chief told Moise to get up. Blood ran freely from his body. Moise walked around and shook hands with everyone, including Charlo. The next day the sheriff came to Charlo's camp to arrest Moise for the murder, but Charlo told him the crime had already been paid for.

Antoine Moise took part in one of the most famous battles fought by the Flatheads against their enemies, out on the buffalo plains. The Flathead party consisted of about 80 hunters, led by their war chief, Arlee. This took place around the year 1860, not far from the present Crow Reservation, in Eastern Montana.

While searching for Buffalo herds the Flatheads came across the fresh trail of many people. They thought these tracks were made by River Crows, in whose country they were. Instead, the tracks had been made by Mountain Crows, fleeing from a large war party of Sioux. These Crows had recently killed a number of Soux, whose relatives were out looking for revenge.

That night the Flatheads camped not far from where they had seen the tracks. The next morning they awoke just in time to see several strangers making off with some of the Flathead horses. A few Flatheads took off after the horse-thieves, who turned out to be Sioux. During the wild chase which followed, four of the Sioux were killed and most of the horses recovered. Then, as the Flatheads rounded a bend in the river, they found themselves at the edge of a huge Sioux encampment.

ABOVE:Chief Antoine Moise (seated) and his friend Magpie, c. 1910.

The Coup of Sam Resurrection

One of the more colorful individuals among the Flathead-Salish in the early 1900s was Sam Resurrection, an old warrior and buffalo hunter. An interesting experience led to his unusual last name.

Very sick as a young boy, medicine men finally gave up trying to save him. When he stopped breathing, his parents mourned and prepared for a funeral. His mother took a new woollen blanket and made nice leggings to dress him for the final journey. But when she started to put them on him, he opened his eyes and looked at her. She screamed, and others came running. For the rest of his life, Sam Resurrection liked to tell about the trick he played to get a new pair of leggings from his mother!

As a tribal elder, he was once sent to Washington, D.C. When his interpreter ran off, he went ahead anyway, using his poor English combined with sign language. He managed to convince politicians to give the tribe money that he had been sent to obtain. The people looked at him with awe for having been so effective in the big, far-away city.

The following adventure was told by him in the 1930's and recorded by H.H. Turney-High:

"A long time ago when I was young a party of us Salish went North and East to the plains to hunt buffalo. We were camping near the site of the present town of Browning one night. The next morning it was discovered that someone had stolen some of the horses and it seemed from the tracks that it was the work of three men. We friends promptly decided to give chase on the remaining horses to discover what tribe the thieves had belonged to, and to recover our property if we could. We travelled all that day and all the next night. This the enemy did not do, for they turned out to be Blackfoot . . . .

"We were able to surprise these Blackfoot. Two of them succeeded in galloping away, but I got quite close to the third before he realized his fix. I galloped close to him, and the Blackfoot took his bow from the case and strung it. Because he was in such a hurry he did a poor job and the bowstring slipped off. This gave me a chance which I took, galloping up to count *coup* on the enemy. I whipped him in the face time and time again with my riding quirt, then I wrested the bow from his hand. Coming to grips we two galloped over the plain wrestling, each trying to throw the other to the ground. In this struggle I removed the man's bow-case and arrow-quiver. At this time, the Salish friends overtook us, and the Blackfoot was thrown to the ground.

"The chief then said, 'let us not kill him now but take all his property away from him.' This gave the others the chance to count *coups* on the Piegan. The chief counted *coup* first by striking the man in the face with his quirt. Then two of the others did the same. One man could not count *coup* as he remained mounted to guard us from the other Piegans who might be in the neighbourhood. A fifth man, a warrior named Ka-no, was enabled to count *coup* because he stripped the fine Hudson's Bay blanket from the Blackfoot.

"The chief then said, 'Let us not kill him, but let us punish him by leaving him here in the winter storm naked so that he will freeze,' and we did that. All those who had counted *coup* on the Blackfoot then notched their sticks. That was the first time I ever counted *coup*, and that is what this feather stands for."

ABOVE: Sam Resurrection, c. 1915

The direction of the chase suddenly changed, as the Flatheads tried to return to the rest of their party. A large number of Sioux came after them on fresh horses and managed to kill several Flatheads, before the rest reached their camp. Within a short time the Flathead camp was surrounded by the Sioux party, which was estimated to numer more that 1,000 men.

The Flathead camp was, fortunately, well protected. The Sioux force was unable to storm the camp, although they managed to kill 18 Flatheads and wound many others during the day-long battle. The Flathead hunters were well-armed with rifles. They killed 24 of the Sioux.

The battle ended after sundown, when most of the Sioux returned to their camp. They knew the Flatheads were trapped, so they left only enough of their men behind to keep the Flatheads surrounded until morning. However, the Flatheads knew the country so well that they found an escape route which was not protected by the confident Sioux. They even managed to escape with all their horses and wounded men. By morning they had travelled so far that the Sioux were unable to catch up, although they tried. It was later learned that the pursuing Siox passed close by two other Flathead hunting camps—both of them very small and vulnerable. However, neither side knew this at the time.

104

Stories of Daily Life
Told by Victor Vanderburg in 1935.

Victor Vanderburg was born in the Bitterroot Valley back when life was still very good there. As a boy he often accompanied his people out to the plains when they went Buffalo hunting. Because of these experiences he became one of the tribe's foremost historians in his later years. He was also a close friend and advisor to Chief Martin Charlo. Victor's father, Louis Vanderburg, lived to be 104 years old. He was the last survivor of those who had signed the Treaty in 1855. In 1884 he accompanied Charlo to Washington, D.C. and tried to pursuade the government to let his people remain in the Bitterroot Valley. Many knew him by his old name, Far-Away-Grizzly-Bear. Others knew him as Louis. It is said he adopted the last name of Vanderburg to honour one of the early settlers in the Bitterroot Valley. Louis Vanderburg raised his son, Victor, in the old-time Flathead way, and never sent him to the mission school. This is how Victor described a typical day among the Flatheads back in those times.

He said the camp was usually awakened before daybreak by the chief's crier. After arising, most of the people went right down to the river to take their morning baths. The young men were sent to untie the horses near the lodge and take them out from the camp so they could graze. Children were also sent down to bathe in the river. When they came back, they were covered up until they warmed up, but they were not allowed to stand by the fire.

BELOW: Flathead-Salish Tipi Camp, c. 1925   (McKay Photo)

Breakfast was eaten very early—often before sunrise. Girls would be sent out for firewood, after which they helped their mothers cook. The meal was usually prepared with dried meat, camas, bitterroots, and berries. If there was any fresh meat, it was boiled. This was done by digging a hole in the ground and spreading a bull buffalo hide over the hole. The hole was filled with water and fresh meat. Red hot stones were then dropped into the water until the meat boiled. The people drank the broth and ate the meat. Hot food was placed in bowls made of wood or shaped from horn, or placed on green leaves or grass. Afterward, the household was cleaned and swept with a broom of branches by the girls of the family.

The people always camped in a circle back then, in a place determined by the chief. His relatives camped next to him. Spaces between the lodges were fixed up so the horses could not leave the camp circle during the night. If other tribes camped with the Flatheads they usually followed their own style of camping. For instance, Victor said the Pend d'Oreille would put up their tipis anywhere, sometimes occupying empty places left in the Flathead camp circle. If several tribes combined to go buffalo hunting they acted as one tribe, usually under the Flathead head chief. The chief always met with his council of minor chiefs before camp was moved. Their decisions were then announced to the people by the chief's crier.

A chief's council was always opened by the smoking of the chief's pipe. He filled the pipe, lit it, the passed it to his left. The men were seated in the council according to their rank. If head chiefs from other tribes were present they always sat next to the Flathead leader. Behind the pipe was passed a buffalo horn cup from which each smoker took a drink of water.

BELOW: Flathead leaders at a council meeting in Dixon, c. 1920. From right to left, standing: Head Chief Martin Charlo; Jerome Vanderburg; government inspector Coleman; Paul Antoine; Antoine Felix; Phillip Cullooyah; Elizabeth Charlo; Sam Resurrection; Michel One Night. Seated, right to left: Joe La Mousse; Louie Vanderburg; Antoine Moise; Louie Pierre; John Charlie; Uustah (with pipe); Pascal Antoine; Michel Stevens.

106

The special pipe used for smoking at council meetings belonged to the head chief. Upon his death it was passed to his eldest son, or to whomever succeeded him. There is a place in Phillipsburg Valley where red stone was found for making pipes. A blueish stone for pipes was found near Boulder, Montana. Fire showed through these stone pipes when they were lit.

After breakfast, women of the household began their duties for the day. These included slicing meat to dry, scraping and tanning hides, and pounding dried meat. There was always sewing and mending to be done — mocassins, clothing, or tipi covers.

If the family had a baby it was taken out of its buffalo-hide bag before breakfast and placed on a robe so that it could move its arms and legs for a while. Later it was washed and placed in a cradle board for the day. Moss was placed at the bottom of the cradle board bag in place of a diaper. One of the younger girls in the family would look after the baby while it was awake. When it fell asleep the cradle board was leaned against one of the tipi poles or hung from a tree branch.

Youngsters of the family hauled water from the stream in round-bottomed rawhide bags. The girls brought in enough firewood to last until late afternoon, when they went out for the night's supply. If there was no other work to be done, children could go out to play at this time.

During the winter, the men spent much of their time in camp, taking care of horses, working on weapons and tools, or just sitting together to talk and smoke. While visiting, some of the men would be busy making horn cups and spoons, hair ropes, quivers, and other items. If anyone become hungry during the day they helped themselves to some of the dried meat.

The evening meal was held just before sunset. It was prepared in the same way as breakfast. Some methods of cooking were boiling, roasting and broiling. There were two popular ways of roasting meat, as follows:

The most common was to spear a piece of meat on a stake that was about two or three feet long. The stake was set in the ground near the fire until the meat was done.

The other method involved the use of an earth oven, also described in the preparartion of camas. Red hot rocks were placed in the bottom of a rectangular pit. These were covered with small logs, over which was placed a layer of pine boughs. Pieces of meat were layed on top of the boughs and covered with more boughs, then a layer of green grass. Finally, earth from the pit was piled over the whole affair and left for a day. After that time the meat was thoroughly roasted.

Food was boiled in hide-covered holes, as mentioned earlier. As soon as the food was ready it was removed and the hide taken up to keep it from becoming water soaked. the hole was located to the left or right of the lodge entrance. In summer, it was usually located outdoors. This method of cooking was not much used after kettles were obtained from traders.

When the people finished eating they cleaned their hands by passing them through their hair. They only washed their hands with water if they had eaten fish. This custom was opposite to that of neighbours further West (where fish were much more important to the diet.) Those people washed their hands after eating meat, passing them through the hair only after eating fish.

Fire was made with the use of a plam drill, set into a piece of rotted cottonwood. Several people took turns twirling the stick before the tinder at its base caught fire. At night, coals of the fire were covered with ashes so they would still be glowing in the morning. If the fire had gone out by then, glowing coals were brought from another lodge.

107

ABOVE: Victor Vanderburg, c. 1920.

Hunting

For Flathead men of the past, the most important activity in a typical day was hunting. During Summer and Fall, when the people often camped out on the plains, men went out hunting nearly every day. These hunting trips were usually done communally, so that none went out ahead to frighten the herds, and everyone obtainedat least some meat.

The hunting party was led by the hunting chief, elected by the people on the basis of his skill as a hunter. He would send scouts ahead to locate the buffalo herds. The hunters would follow, riding their pack horses and leading their special hunting mounts. The head chief generally remained in camp to protect the rest of his people. With him remained ten "policemen," specially chosen by him. These men kept order in the camp, prevented its members from wandering off to scare buffalo or attract enemies, and defended the camp in case of attack. Friends and relatives of the head chief, and his men, brought them shares of meat.

Once buffalo were sighted, the hunters mounted their fast horses. The preferred weapons were bows and arrows, as these could be fired faster than guns. The hunting chief rode his horse in a zigzag manner in front of the hunters so that none might get ahead to alarm the buffalo. Behind the hunters would ride some widows, who came along to seek their own portions of meat — given out of generosity by relatives and others who wished to be kind.

A hunter would gallop towards the buffalo herd and approach one so as to come up even with its left side. Fat cow buffalo were favoured for their tender meat, if there was a choice of animals. Cow hides were also thinner and easier to tan than a bull's. If possible, the hunter shot two buffalo before he gave up the hunt. He tried to keep his buffalo close to other killed ones, so that the hunters would not be too spread out in case of enemy attack.

Each man would skin and cut up the animals that he shot. He began by removing the hide with his knife. Then he cut off the lower legs. These were broken up and boiled, at home, for the precious marrow which they contained. Next, he removed the two large pieces of sinew that lie along the backbone. These were dried and made into thread for sewing. He cut a chunk off each side of the shoulder, to take home for immediate roasting. Finally, the hunter removed the tongue and heart, which was left attached to the kidneys. After that he would quarter and butcher the rest of the carcass.

Victor said a good pack horse could easily carry back to camp all that a Flathead hunter took from a typical buffalo. Rawhide thongs were passed througfh holes cut into each of the quarters. These were then slung in pairs across the pack horse's back. Long slabs of meat from the under and upper part of the body were balanced over the quarters. The heavy, wet hide was thrown over all the meat.

While the hunter was still in the field, he could give away part or all of what he had shot to widows or poor people. They would then go and butcher what was given to them. But once he was back home and turned the meat over to his wife, he no longer had any say about it.

The hunter and his wife reminded their children not to make fun of the buffalo or any of the parts. Spirits of the buffalo would cause trouble for the one who was so thoughtless. Victor once knew an old man named Tama to whom this had happened, back in the time of Victor's father, Louis.

According to Victor, this man had killed a buffalo bull, one time. His horse had a sore back, so Tama took out the bull's tallow, which was good-sized, and put it on the horse's back as a saddle blanket. He put his saddle on top of it and rode back to camp. A few days later, while the camp was quiet, someone called out, "There is a buffalo bull charging into camp!" The bull ran amongst the tipis until he came to the front of Tama's tipi. When Tama saw that, he crawled out the back of his lodge and ran away to hide. The bull appeared very angry and kicked dust all over Tama's lodge. Several men from the camp attacked the bull and managed to kill him, after many shots. It fell on the tipi next to Tama's. Everyone in camp scolded Tama for his failure to respect the buffalo that he had killed a few days before.

Another buffalo hunting story told by Victor concerned the famous Flathead "holy man," Bear Track, baptized by the missionaries and also named Alexander. He had the "power" to leave his body and transport his Spirit to other places, then return and report to the people what he had seen. His specialty was going out and calling buffalo to come towards the Flathead hunters.

One year in the time of Victor's father, the people moved out on the plains in the Fall to hunt, but they could find no buffalo herds. They asked Bear Track to use his "power." Bear Track had several tipis fastened side by side, so that the people could all join in his ceremony. During the first night he only sang the Power songs of his medicine.

The second night Bear Track called all the people to come and dance, while he sang more of his "Medicine songs." The words in the first songs were: "The white buffalo cow is getting herself ready."

People were standing around Bear Track in a circle, jumping up and down in time to his singing. He appointed one woman to dance out in front of the group, wearing a buffalo hide which covered her head. She stooped down and imitated a cow buffalo, while the others made buffalo noises. Bear Track kept time to his singing with a long pole, to the top of which were tied a bunch of hooves that rattled.

After some time, Bear Track sang out: "Now, the white buffalo cow is coming towards us, and other buffalo are stringing out behind her." His voice was calling out what his Spirit was seeing.

A while later Bear Track continued his vision, saying: "Just about daybreak this white cow will pass us by. She'll be leading the other buffalo. Just let them go and let another day go by, then there will be plenty of buffalo all around us to hunt and kill." He also said that one of the first buffalo to be killed would fall dead right at the spot where the dance was going on.

During the whole time of this ceremony, while Bear Track was having his vision, a blizzard was raging outside. It did not stop until just before daybreak. The people kept on dancing. Soon someone shouted, "Buffalo are seen coming this way." Bear Track called on the people to take down the special tipi and to watch for the buffalo.

As the buffalo came near camp, a minor chief named Ambrose prepared to go out and hunt them. His sons prepared to follow him. Ambrose was a faithful Catholic who had little respect for Bear Track's traditional "powers." People tried to talk Ambrose out of going ahead, but when they saw that he would not listen they decided to join him, rather than take a chance on having Ambrose scare all the buffalo away before they could get any.

They rode into the buffalo herd and the animals separated. A small bunch was cut off and killed by the hunters, but most of the herd turned back and fled. Chief Charlo chased one cow right into camp and shot her so that she dropped dead right at the place where the Medicine Dance had been held the night before.

ABOVE: Mary Kiser shows how to hold Elk meat while cutting it up for drying.

BELOW: A Flathead camp in the Bitterroot Valley, near Florence, Montana, c. 1890.

(John Voss Photo, Florence)

111

The people were happy to have buffalo meat again, but angry with Ambrose for scaring most of the herd away. One, a man from the Spokan tribe, said to Ambrose, "You know that all these buffalo did not come here as a result of your kind of praying — they came because of Bear Track's Medicine!"

Many stories are told about Bear Track's "powers," which remained with him even after he became blind, with old age. He died in the Bitterroot Valley not long before the people left from there. Sometimes he would decorate his horse and himself according to his dreams, then ride around the camp. He had a red wool mask with a pair of bufalo horns which he would tie over his horse's head. Then he would put on his buckskin suit, special feather headdress, and paint on his face. He would accept no payments for using his "powers." He would say, "It was just to help out the people."

After the return from Summer and Fall buffalo hunting, the men would go out to hunt deer and and elk whenever fresh meat was needed in the household. A man could do this kind of hunting alone, or with others. Victor's grandfather told him a favourite method for success with this kind of hunting. He would go to a place where there was a natural salt lick. He would hide there and wait until some elk came to lick the salt. These places were usually way out in the open, so he could not get close enough to have a shot at the elk. Instead, he would follow the elk when they left. He would stay on their tracks until he figured out that they had gone into a brush to lie down and rest. Then he would approach from the windward side, take off his clothes, and crawl up until he was close enough for a sure shot. First he would shoot one and then another one as it rose to its feet. Victor often used this method that his grandfather taught him.

Victor used another method of getting close to elk. In the fall, when the animals were mating, he would make a whistle from the stalk of the cow parsnip. He would cut the stalk so that one of the closed joints was at the end of his whistle. He cut the mouthpiece end into a point and inserted a flat reed into it. By blowing and moving the tongue in the right way he was able to make sounds that attracted elk and deer.

Victor said that he cut up elk the same way as buffalo. He would pile all the butchered meat on the ground and cover it with the animal's skin. Then he would walk back to camp for a pack horse. He would lay his gun case or something else that carried his odour on top of the piled meat, to keep away other animals, like bears and wolves.

When Victor was a boy he used to snare a lot of birds, like grouse and prairie chicken. Men only did this in emergencies, but they encouraged boys to learn hunting skills in this way. The favourite time for trapping these birds was in the Spring. At that time they gather in groups and hold mating dances during the night. They dance each night in the same place. Victor would set up a number of loop snares made from sinew thread. The birds would get their feet or heads caught in the loops.

Victor also used to catch woodchucks and gophers with snares, either by setting them over the animals' holes, or by holding them at the end of a long stick. Like birds, the animals were roasted whenever the boys brought them home to their mothers.

Victor said the people used to catch fish, in the old days, but they never depended upon them as a food source. Most fishing was done through the ice in winter. Fishing line was woven from the hair of a horse's tail. A piece was cut from a thorn bush to make the hook. This piece had a thorn sticking out to one side and a stem to serve as the shank. The stem was attached to the woven hair line with sinew. The sinew also served as a belt.

Louie Ninepipe

Noted Dancer and Singer

Louie Ninepipe was one of the last Flatheads living on the reservation but born in the Bitterroots. He was a friendly man, with an honest and colorful personality. Into the 1970s, when he was past eighty, his presence in the circle of drummers added character to each pow-wow. He figured he had attended over a thousand dances and pow-wows in his lifetime!

For many years the "Ninepipe brothers" were noted as top-rate singers and drummers at Indian events all over the Northwest, especially around the Rockies. Everyone seemed to agree that they were the most talented group on the Flathead reservation. They always came dressed in their beautiful beaded outfits, so that they could join the dancers when others were singing.

Two of Louie's brothers—Adolf and Andrew—shared his traditional lifestyle and activities until old age, into the 1950s. Adolf's good humour and warm personality caused him to be nicknamed "Happy" Ninepipe. Andrew, on the other hand, was quiet and serious, greatly respected by the people for his medicinal and spiritual knowledge.

Their father was Antoine Ninepipe, a good buffalo hunter, later a successful farmer. Among his notable exploits was one in which a Flathead hunting party was overwhelmed by Sioux warriors out on the Plains and he helped defend his people, though suffering from a gunshot in the leg. His father, Joseph Ninepipe, was among those Flatheads who welcomed the first priests and settlers into the Bitterroot Valley, innocently thinking there was enough room for all.

Louie and his brothers used two kinds of drums to accompany their singing. The most popular traditional style was the "hand drum," made by stretching a piece of rawhide across a wooden hoop about 18 inches in diameter. Several men would stand in a circle and beat their drums in unison, while singing.

For public dances Louie also had a large drum, about three feet across. Six or eight men would sit around it and beat at the same time. These are the most common drums seen at pow-wows today. Modern bass drums are often used in place of Indian-made ones.

Louie was also good at playing the traditional Flathead flute, or flageolette, an instrument mostly used for love songs. Originally these flutes were made from partly-dried Elderberry wood. This has a soft center which is easily punched out. A slit was made at the upper end and partially stopped up with pine pitch or gum. There were two sets of three holes, plus a seventh hole that was not played. Some were nearly two feet long, while others were much shorter. In his old age, Louie had two flutes made from sawed-off pieces of rifle barrel. He surprised first-time listeners with the beautiful sounds they made.

"War dancing" was Louie's favorite activity, though it involved only fun and excitement, not the practice of war. Yet many of his early fellow dancers were retired warriors, a couple generations older than he, who had participated in actual war dances before heading out to battle. In those days dancers carried weapons and imitated actions from the warpath, such as scouting, sneaking up, stabbing, shooting, and acting proud or brave.

War dances were preceded by the traditional Flathead Snake dance, in Louie's younger days when these events were usually held outdoors, by tipi camps. Then men would all go down by the river and get dressed up in their costumes. When ready, they danced back into camp in a long, weaving line, like a snake. Singers and drummers followed the dancers, with women and children dancing behind them. One of Louie's relatives was for a long time the Snake dance leader.

113

Not only did the Snake dance precede the War dance, but a special parade also had to take place ahead of all that. In the mornings all the people would dress up in their best clothing and decorate their horses with beadwork and bells. The riders gathered outside the camp circle, then rode in from the East. A prominent man led the single file of riders as they went around inside the camp circle in the same direction as the Sun. They made four trips around, each time going a little faster. At the end they all raced to the place where the dance was to be held, dismounted, and began dancing. This must have been a spectacle of sight and sound!

The social dance that Louie was most familiar with is called the Round Dance, Gift Dance, or Squaw Dance. He said it came from the Sioux not long after he and the last of Charlo's people moved to the reservation in 1891. The dance starts out with women forming a large circle and dancing clockwise, moving their feet sideways in a hitching step, keeping time to the drumming and singing. The singers usually stand in the center of the circle, facing the dancers. If they are using hand drums, singers often stand back to back and turn along with the dancers. A large space is left between the singers and the dancers, with the dancers often singing along.

Once the dance gets started women go around and choose men to join them as partners. The woman can be from the audience as well as from the dance circle. The couples go out to the open space in the center and dance in the same way and direction as the circle of women. The couples hold hands, or put their arms around each other.

When the song for that dance is over, the women sit down and the announcer steps into the circle. He goes to each woman and asks what kind of gift she is going to give her partner. He then calls out the name of the woman and holds up her gift, or says what it is, before he gives it to her partner. The gift might be a nice scarf, some money, or tobacco. In former times, blankets, horses and beadwork were frequent gifts.

Joking, teasing and other merriment was common at this time, while jealousy was also known. For the next dance, it was the men who chose partners. Usually they picked the same women who had chosen them, and when it came time for gifts, they gave something of like value, or better.

BELOW: Louie Ninepipe (waving), with his brothers Andrew (left) and Adolf Ninepipe

ABOVE: Louie Ninepipe, at home in the Jocko Valley, 1967. (AHW Photo)

The story of Louie Ninepipe would not be complete without a mention of traditional Flathead "love medicine," which led to a final, notable event in his life. The story begins with Eneas Three Heads, who received some "love medicine" while out alone on a hunting trip in the Jocko Valley.

Three Heads had stopped to rest, when he fell asleep. During that time, he heard very nice-sounding music coming from somewhere in the distance. Then he saw some little insects with shiny wings flying towards him. One of the insects told him: "We are the ones making all that music you hear. We use flutes, rattles, bells and drums. We can perform all kinds of wonderful things with our music, and from now on you will be able to do the same. We will teach you a song to play. You will have to make a flute just like the ones you see us using. When you play this song you will be able to have any woman that you want, no matter who she is or how far away she lives. You have to play this song often and think very hard about the woman that you want. We will come and take that song into that woman's mind. Pretty soon she will start thinking about you, until she can't think about anything else. You can give this song to someone else and it will work for him in the same way."

Eneas Three Heads was said to have used this song successfully and taught it to his friend, Pierre Pichette, who was Louie's stepfather. Pichette was a wise man who remembered many things he learned during his long life. Blind since youth, he was encouraged by a white judge to become historian of his tribe. Louie learned many things from his stepfather, including the potent "love song."

In his old age, Louie was sometimes lonesome, having lost his lifelong family and friends. He said he wanted one more sweetheart, so he put the love music to test.

A young lady in England heard a record album of Flathead songs recorded by Louie and others, and through this she started to send him letters. The test proved positive; soon she began sending candies and perfumed envelopes! One day she appeared in nearby Missoula on a bus, from which Louie brought her to the Justice of Peace, where they were promptly married. Newspaper headlines proclaimed it a "fairytale wedding." He lived in near bliss for his final couple of years, pampered by a lovely young lass, until he died in 1974.

* * * * *

Time and Seasons

Back when the people spent most of their lives outdoors they always knew what part of the day it was by looking at the position of the sun. Victor said there used to be names for the different parts of the day. The morning began with the "First Light," which was just before dawn. "Light coming on Earth" was the time of dawn. "Sun in plain sight" was the time after sunrise. " Sun directly above" was noon. Later came "Sunset," then the time "Before darkness."

At night the passing of time was marked by the positions of various constellations — especially the Big Dipper. The only part of the night with a special name was "Midnight."

Months were known as Moons — the time it takes for one cycle of the moon is just about the same as the passing of a month. The moon was called the "Night Sun." The year began in mid-winter, when the sun reached the furthest South and the moon reached the furthest North. At that time the people would say, "now the moon is returning." This period was called the "Middle of Winter Moon."

When the next moon began mothers would tell their children to go outside and say: "Audla, audla, audla, audla." The meaning of the word has been forgotten, but the children would point at the moon with their hands and say that word to make this cold moon (January) pass quickly.

March was called the "Moon when the wild geese come." Their arrival meant that Spring was soon behind. The period around May was called "Moon in which Bitterroot is dug." The "Mid-Summer Moon" was around the middle of July, when plants and grasses were about full grown. Around September was the "Moon of wild Cherries," when Chokecherries were gathered and dried.

In the time of Victor's grandfather the people still gathered each year for a Mid-Summer Festival of Thanksgiving. His granfather showed him the place where this ceremony was always held. It was about seven miles above Hamilton, Montana, and was called "Dancing Place." The head chief led all his people as they danced in a circle around a large shade tree. Men and women alternated in the dance line, and everyone wore an eagle feather to symbolize the mightiest of birds.

As the people danced around in the circle they followed each other and swung their right arms in time to the drumming. They danced by jumping off the ground with both feet. Different people sang their Medicine songs for the people to dance by. At the end of each song the people would stop and raise their right hands towards the sun and pray:

"Hi-Yo Sun — far away . . . . help me to be well — not to get sick . . . . and also my children — always to be well and not to get sick."

Then the people would lower their hands towards the Earth and pray, asking for continued food and good health. Although Flathead people never adopted the complex Sun Dance ceremonies from tribes of the Plains, this Mid-Summer Thanksgiving ceremony was their own version of it.

The people kept track of the passing of the moons, and especially years, by placing beads on special strings, or by making notches on a bone hide scraper. Some tied knots to a long string, which was kept rolled in a ball. Some women added a bead for each year to the fringes at the front of buckskin dresses which were kept throughout their life-times. The years were named according to some outstanding event - like the death of a chief, a particular victory, or a hard winter.

Recent Statistics of the Confederated Salish and Kutenai Tribes of the Flathead Reservation

 1.2 million acres within reservation boundaries.

 6,500 enrolled tribal members, about 3,800 living on the reservation.

Tribal Economy includes logging, post & pole operation, Family farming, & ranching, construction, recreation, electrical utility distribution, BIA irrigation work; about 500 people employed by the tribe.

BELOW: Flatheads in Missoula, c. 1900   (Howell Studio)

ABOVE: Flathead winter camp in the Bitterroots, c. 1890.

Flathead-Salish Bibliography

Curtis, Edward S., *The North American Indian*, Vol.7, Norwood, Massachusetts, 1911.

Merriam, Allan P., *Ethnomusicology of the Flathead Indians*, New York: Wenner-Gren Foundation for Anthropological Research, 1967.

Ronan, Major Peter, *Historical Sketch of the Flathead Indian Nation*, Helena: Journal Publishing Co., 1890.

Schaeffer, Claude S., *Unpublished field notes taken among the Flatheads between 1935 and 1960.* American Museum of Natural History, New York, and Glenbow-Alberta Institute Archives, Calgary.

Teit, J.A. (F. Boas, ed.), *The Salishan Tribes of the Western Plateaus.* Washington: Fourth-Fifth Annual Report of the Bureau of American Ethnology, 1930.

Turney-High, H.H., *The Flathead Indians of Montana.* Menasha: American Anthropological Association Memoir 56, 1937.

The Full Blood Flathead Indian Montana Study Group. Mimeographed papers from 1947, at Montana State University, Missoula.

118

Pikunni - Blackfeet at Running Eagle Falls,   Glacier National Park, 1913. (Marble Photo)

TREATIES

Signed by
Tribes of the Northern Rockies

1855 U.S. TREATY WITH BLACKFEET

Articles of agreement and convention made and concluded between the United States and the Blackfeet and other tribes of Indians, at the council ground on the Upper Missouri River, October 17, 1855.

Articles of agreement and convention made and concluded at the council ground on the Upper Missouri, near the mouth of the Judith River, in the Territory of Nebraska, this 17th day of October, in the year 1855, by and between A. Cumming and Isaac I. Stevens, commissioners duly appointed and authorized on the part of the United States, and the undersigned chiefs, headmen, and delegates of the following nations and tribes of Indians, who occupy, for the purposes of hunting, the territory on the Upper Missouri and Yellowstone Rivers, and who have permanent homes as follows : East of the Rocky Mountains the Blackfeet Nation, consisting of the Piegan, Blood, Blackfeet, and Gros Ventres tribes of Indians ; west of the Rocky Mountains the Flathead Nation, consisting of the Flathead, Upper Pend d'Oreille, and Kootenay tribes of Indians, and the Nez Percé tribes of Indians ; the said chiefs, headmen, and delegates, in behalf of and acting for said nations and tribes, and being duly authorized thereto by them.

ARTICLE I. Peace, friendship, and amity, shall hereafter exist between the United States and the aforesaid nations and tribes of Indians, parties to this treaty, and the same shall be perpetual.

ARTICLE II. The aforesaid nations and tribes of Indians, parties to this treaty, do hereby jointly and severally covenant that peaceful relations shall likewise be maintained among themselves in future ; and that they will abstain from all hostilities whatsoever against each other, and cultivate mutual good will and friendship. And the nations and tribes aforesaid do furthermore jointly and severally covenant that peaceful relations shall be maintained with and that they will abstain from all hostilities whatsoever, excepting in self-defense, against the following named nations and tribes of Indians, to wit: the Crows, Assinaboines, Crees, Snakes, Blackfeet, Sans Arce, and Aunce-pa-pas bands of Sioux, and all other neighboring nations and tribes of Indians.

ARTICLE III. The Blackfeet Nation consent and agree that all that portion of the country recognized and defined by the treaty of Laramie as Blackfeet territory, lying within lines drawn from the Hell Gate or Medicine Rock Passes in the main range of the Rocky Mountains, in an easterly direction to the nearest source of the Muscleshell River, thence to the mouth of Twenty-five Yard Creek, thence up the Yellowstone River to its northern source, and thence along the main range of the Rocky Mountains, in a northerly direction, to the point of beginning, shall be a common hunting ground for ninety-nine years, where all the nations, tribes, and bands of Indians, parties to this treaty, may enjoy equal and uninterrupted privileges of hunting, fishing. and gathering fruit, grazing animals, curing meat, and dressing robes. They further agree that they will not establish villages, or in any other way exercise exclusive rights within ten miles of the northern line of the common hunting ground, and that the parties to this treaty may hunt on said northern boundary line and within ten miles thereof: *Provided*, That the western Indians, parties to this treaty, may hunt on the trail leading down the Muscle-shell to the Yellowstone ; the Muscleshell River being the boundary separating the Blackfeet from the Crow territory : *And provided*, That no nation, band, or tribe of Indians, parties to this treaty, nor any other Indians, shall be permitted to establish permanent settlements, or in any other way exercise, during the period above mentioned, exclusive rights or privileges within the limits of the above described hunting ground : *And provided further*, That the rights of the western Indians to a whole or a part of the common hunting ground, derived from occupancy and possession, shall not be affected by this article, except so far as said rights may be determined by the treaty of Laramie.

ARTICLE IV. The parties to this treaty agree and consent that the tract of country lying within lines drawn from the Hell Gate or Medicine Rock Passes, in an easterly direction, to the nearest source of the Muscleshell River, thence down said river to its mouth, thence down the channel of the Missouri River to the mouth of Milk River, thence due north to the forty-ninth parallel, thence due west on said parallel to the main range of the Rocky Mountains, and thence southerly along said range to the place of beginning, shall be the territory of the Blackfeet Nation, over which said nation shall exercise exclusive control, excepting as may be otherwise provided in this treaty ; subject, however, to the provisions of the third article of this treaty, giving the right to hunt, and prohibiting the establishment of permanent villages and the exercise of any exclusive rights within ten miles of the northern line of the common hunting ground, drawn from the nearest source of the Muscleshell River to the Medicine Rock Passes, for the period of ninety-nine years : *Provided also*, That the Assinaboines shall have the right of hunting, in common with the Blackfeet, in the country lying between the aforesaid eastern boundary line, running from the mouth of Milk River to the forty-ninth parallel, and a line drawn from the left bank of the Missouri River, opposite the Round Butte, north to the forty-ninth parallel.

121

ARTICLE V. The parties to this treaty residing west of the main range of the Rocky Mountains agree and consent that they will not enter the common hunting ground, nor any part of the Blackfeet territory, or return home by any pass in the main range of the Rocky Mountains to the north of the Hell Gate or Medicine Rock Passes. And they further agree that they will not hunt or otherwise disturb the game when visiting the Blackfeet territory for trade or social intercourse.

ARTICLE VI. The aforesaid nations and tribes of Indians, parties to this treaty, agree and consent to remain within their own respective countries, except when going to or from, or whilst hunting upon, the "common hunting ground," or when visiting each other for the purpose of trade or social intercourse.

ARTICLE VII. The aforesaid nations and tribes of Indians agree that citizens of the United States may live in and pass unmolested through the countries respectively occupied and claimed by them. And the United States is hereby bound to protect said Indians against depredations and other unlawful acts which white men residing in or passing through their country may commit.

ARTICLE VIII. For the purpose of establishing traveling thoroughfares through their country, and the better to enable the President to execute the provisions of this treaty, the aforesaid nations and tribes do hereby consent and agree that the United States may, within the countries respectively occupied and claimed by them, construct roads of every description; establish lines of telegraph and military posts; use materials of every description found in the Indian country; build houses for agencies, missions, schools, farms, shops, mills, stations, and for any other purpose for which they may be required, and permanently occupy as much land as may be necessary for the various purposes above enumerated, including the use of wood for fuel and land for grazing, and that the navigation of all lakes and streams shall be forever free to citizens of the United States.

ARTICLE IX. In consideration of the foregoing agreements, stipulations, and cessions, and on condition of their faithful observance, the United States agree to expend, annually, for the Piegan, Blood, Blackfeet, and Gros Ventres tribes of Indians, constituting the Blackfeet Nation, in addition to the goods and provisions distributed at the time of signing this treaty, $20,000 annually for ten years, to be expended in such useful goods and provisions, and other articles as the President, at his discretion, may, from time to time, determine; and the superintendent or other proper officer shall each year inform the President of the wishes of the Indians in relation thereto: *Provided, however,* That if, in the judgment of the President and Senate, this amount be insufficient it may be increased not to exceed the sum of $35,000 per year.

ARTICLE X. The United States further agree to expend annually, for the benefit of the aforesaid tribes of the Blackfeet Nation, a sum not exceeding $15,000 annually for ten years, in establishing and instructing them in agricultural and mechanical pursuits, and in educating their children, and in any other respect promoting their civilization and christianization: *Provided, however,* That, to accomplish the objects of this article, the President may, at his discretion, apply any or all the annuities provided for in this treaty: *And provided also,* That the President may, at his discretion, determine in what proportions the said annuities shall be divided among the several tribes.

ARTICLE XI. The aforesaid tribes acknowledge their dependence on the Government of the United States, and promise to be friendly with all citizens thereof, and to commit no depredations or other violence upon such citizens. And should any one or more violate this pledge, and the fact be proved to the satisfaction of the President, the property taken shall be returned, or, in default thereof, or if injured or destroyed, compensation may be made by the Government out of the annuities. The aforesaid tribes are hereby bound to deliver such offenders to the proper authorities for trial and punishment, and are held responsible in their tribal capacity to make reparation for depredations so committed. Nor will they make war upon any other tribes, except in self-defense, but will submit all matters of difference between themselves and other Indians to the Government of the United States, through its agent, for adjustment, and will abide thereby. And if any of the said Indians, parties to this treaty, commit depredations on any other Indians within the jurisdiction of the United States, the same rule shall prevail as that prescribed in this article in case of depredations against citizens. And the said tribes agree not to shelter or conceal offenders against the laws of the United States, but to deliver them up to the authorities for trial.

ARTICLE XII. It is agreed and understood by and between the parties to this treaty, that if any nation or tribe of Indians aforesaid shall violate any of the agreements, obligations, or stipulations herein contained, the United States may withhold, for such length of time as the President and Congress may determine, any portion or all of the annuities agreed to be paid to said nation or tribe under the ninth and tenth articles of this treaty.

ARTICLE XIII. The nations and tribes of Indians parties to this treaty, desire to exclude from their country the use of ardent spirits or other intoxicating liquor, and to prevent their people from drinking the same. Therefore it is provided that any Indian belonging to said tribes who is guilty of bringing such liquor into the Indian country, or who drinks liquor, may have his or her proportion of the annuities withheld from him or her for such time as the President may determine.

ARTICLE XIV. The aforesaid nations and tribes of Indians, west of the Rocky Mountains, parties to this treaty, do agree, in consideration of the provisions already made for them in existing treaties, to accept the guarantee of the peaceful occupation of their hunting grounds east of the Rocky Mountains, and of remuneration for depredations made by the other tribes, pledged to be secured to them in this treaty out of the annuities of said tribes, in full compensation for the concessions which they, in common with the said tribes, have made in this treaty.

The Indians east of the mountains, parties to this treaty, likewise recognize and accept the guarantees of this treaty in full compensation for the injuries or depredations which have been or may be committed by the aforesaid tribes west of the Rocky Mountains.

ARTICLE XV. The annuties of the aforesaid tribes shall not be taken to pay the debts of individuals.

ARTICLE XVI. This treaty shall be obligatory upon the aforesaid nations and tribes of Indians parties hereto, from the date hereof, and upon the United States as soon as the same shall be ratified by the President and Senate.

In testimony whereof the said A. Cumming and Isaac I. Stevens, commissioners on the part of the United States, and the undersigned chiefs, headmen, and delegates of the aforesaid nations and tribes of Indians, parties to this treaty, have hereunto set their hands and seals at the place and on the day and year hereinbefore written.

1855 U.S. TREATY WITH FLATHEADS AND KOOTENAYS

Articles of agreement and convention made and concluded at the treaty ground at Hell Gate, in the Bitter Root Valley, this 16th day of July, in the year 1855, by and between Isaac I. Stevens, governor and superintendent of Indian affairs for the Territory of Washington, on the part of the United States, and the undersigned chiefs, headmen, and delegates of the confederated tribes of the Flathead, Kootenay, and Upper Pend d'Oreille Indians, on behalf of and acting for said confederated tribes, and being duly authorized thereto by them. It being understood and agreed that the said confederated tribes do hereby constitute a nation, under the name of the Flathead nation, with Victor, the head chief of the Flathead tribe, as the head chief of the said nation, and that the several chiefs, headmen, and delegates, whose names are signed to this treaty, do hereby, in behalf of their respective tribes, recognize Victor as said head chief.

ARTICLE I. The said confederated tribes of Indians hereby cede, relinquish, and convey to the United States all their right, title, and interest in and to the country occupied or claimed by them, bounded and described as follows, to wit: Commencing on the main ridge of the Rocky Mountains at the forty-ninth parallel of latitude, thence westwardly on the line parallel to the divide between the Flat-bow or Kootenay River and Clarke's Fork ; thence southerly and southeasterly along said divide to the one hundred and fifteenth degree of longitude; thence in a southwesterly direction to the divide between the sources of the Saint Regis Borgia and the Cœur d'Alene Rivers; thence southeasterly and southerly along the main ridge of the Bitter Root Mountains to the divide between the headwaters of the Koos-koos-kee River and of the southwestern fork of the Bitter Root River, thence easterly along the divide separating the waters of the several tributaries of the Bitter Root River from the waters flowing into the Salmon and Snake Rivers, to the main ridge of the Rocky Mountains, and thence northerly along said main ridge to the place of beginning.

ARTICLE II. There is, however, reserved from the lands above ceded, for the use and occupation of the said confederated tribes, and as a general Indian reservation upon which may be placed other friendly tribes and bands of Indians of the Territory of Washington who may agree to be consolidated with the tribes parties to this treaty, under the common designation of the Flathead nation, with Victor, head chief of the Flathead tribe, as the head chief of the nation, the tract of land included within the following boundaries, to wit: Commencing at the source of the main branch of the Jocko River, thence along the divide separating the waters flowing into the Bitter Root River from those flowing into the Jocko to a point on Clarke's Fork between the Camash and Horse prairies; thence northerly to and along the divide bounding on the west the Flathead River to a point due west from the point half way in latitude between the northern and southern extremities of the Flathead Lake; thence on a due east course to the divide whence the Crow, the Prune, the So-ni-el-em, and the Jocko Rivers take their rise, and thence southerly along said divide to the place of beginning; all which tract shall be set apart, and, so far as necessary, surveyed and marked out for the exclusive use and benefit of said confederated tribes as an Indian reservation. Nor shall any white man, excepting those in the employment of the Indian department, be permitted to reside upon the said reservation without permission of the confederated tribes and the superintendent and agent. And the said confederated tribes agree to remove to and settle upon the same within one year after the ratification of this treaty. In the mean time it shall be lawful for them to reside upon any ground not in the actual claim and occupation of citizens of the United States, and upon any ground claimed or occupied if with the permission of the owner or claimant.

Guaranteeing, however, the right to all citizens of the United States to enter upon and occupy as settlers any lands not actually occupied and cultivated by said Indians at this time, and not included in the reservation above named : *And provided*, That any substantial improvements heretofore made by any Indian, such as fields inclosed and cultivated and houses erected upon the lands hereby ceded, and which he may be compelled to abandon in consequence of this treaty, shall be valued under the direction of the President of the United States, and payment made therefor in money, or improvements of an equal value be made for said Indian upon the reservation ; and no Indian will be required to abandon the improvements aforesaid, now occupied by him, until their value in money or improvements of an equal value shall be furnished him as aforesaid.

ARTICLE III. *And provided*, That if necessary for the public convenience roads may be run through the said reservation ; and, on the other hand, the right of way with free access from the same to the nearest public highway is secured to them ; as also the right in common with citizens of the United States to travel upon all public highways.

The exclusive right of taking fish in all the streams running through or bordering said reservation is further secured to said Indians ; as also the right of taking fish at all usual and accustomed places, in common with citizens of the Territory, and of erecting temporary buildings for curing, together with the privilege of hunting, gathering roots and berries, and pasturing their horses and cattle upon open and unclaimed land.

ARTICLE IV. In consideration of the above cession the United States agree to pay to the said confederated tribes of Indians, in addition to the goods and provisions distributed to them at the time of signing this treaty, the sum of $120,000 in the following manner, that is to say : For the first year after the ratification hereof, $36,000, to be expended under the direction of the President in providing for their removal to the reservation, breaking up and fencing farms, building houses for them, and for such other objects as he may deem necessary; for the next four years, $6,000 each year; for the next five years, $5,000 each year; for the next five years, $4,000 each year, and for the next five years, $3,000 each year. All which said sums of money shall be applied to the use and benefit of the said Indians under the direction of the President of the United States, who may from time to time determine, at his discretion, upon what beneficial objects to expend the same for them, and the superintendent of Indian affairs, or other proper officer, shall each year inform the President of the wishes of the Indians in relation thereto.

ARTICLE V. The United States further agree to establish at suitable points within said reservation, within one year after the ratification hereof, an agricultural and industrial school, erecting the necessary buildings, keeping the same in repair, and providing it with furniture, books, and stationery, to be located at the agency, and to be free to the childern of the said tribes, and to employ a suitable instructor or instructors. To furnish one blacksmith shop, to which shall be attached a tin and gun shop, one carpenter's shop, one wagon and plowmaker's shop, and to keep the same in repair and furnished with the necessary tools. To employ two farmers, one blacksmith, one tinner, one gunsmith, one carpenter, one wagon and plowmaker, for the instruction of the Indians in trades, and to assist them in the same. To erect one saw-mill and one flouring-mill, keeping the same in repair and furnished with the necessary tools and fixtures, and to employ two millers. To erect a hospital, keeping the same in repair, and provided with the necessary medicines and furniture, and to employ a physician ; and to erect, keep in repair, and provide with the necessary furniture the buildings required for the accommodation of the said employés. The said buildings and establishments to be maintained and kept in repair as aforesaid, and the employés to be kept in service for the period of twenty years.

And in view of the fact that the head chiefs of the said confederated tribes of Indians are expected and will be called upon to perform many services of a public character, occupying much of their time, the United States further agree to pay to each of the Flathead, Kootenay, and Upper Pend d'Oreille tribes $500 per year, for the term of twenty years after the ratification hereof, as a salary for such persons as the said confederated tribes may select to be their head chiefs, and to build for them at suitable points on the reservation a comfortable house, and properly furnish the same, and to plow and fence for each of them ten acres of land. The salary to be paid to and the said houses to be occupied by such head chiefs as long as they may be elected to that position by their tribes and no longer.

And all the expenditures and expenses contemplated in this article of this treaty shall be defrayed by the United States, and shall not be deducted from the annuities agreed to be paid to said tribes. Nor shall the cost of transporting the goods for the annuity payments be a charge upon the annuities, but shall be defrayed by the United States.

ARTICLE VI. The President may, from time to time, at his discretion, cause the whole, or such portion of such reservation as he may think proper, to be surveyed into lots, and assign the same to such individuals or families of the said confederated tribes as are willing to avail themselves of the privilege, and will locate on the same as a permanent home, on the same terms and subject to the same regulations as are provided in the sixth article of the treaty with the Omahas, so far as the same may be applicable.

ARTICLE VII. The annuities of the aforesaid confederated tribes of Indians shall not be taken to pay the debts of individuals.

ARTICLE VIII. The aforesaid confederated tribes of Indians acknowledge their dependence upon the Government of the United States, and promise to be friendly with all citizens thereof, and pledge themselves to commit no depredations upon the property of such citizens; and should any one or more of them violate this pledge, and the fact be satisfactorily proved before the agent, the property taken shall be returned, or in default thereof, or if injured or destroyed, compensation may be made by the Government out of the annuities. Nor will they make war on any other tribe except in self-defense, but will submit all matters of difference between them and other Indians to the Government of the United States or its agent for decision, and abide thereby; and if any of the said Indians commit any depredations on any other Indians within the jurisdiction of the United States, the same rule shall prevail as that prescribed in this article in case of depredations against citizens; and the said tribe agree not to shelter or conceal offenders against the laws of the United States, but to deliver them up to the authorities for trial.

ARTICLE IX. The said confederated tribes desire to exclude from their reservation the use of ardent spirits, and to prevent their people from drinking the same; and therefore it is provided that any Indian belonging to said confederated tribes of Indians who is guilty of bringing liquor into said reservation, or who drinks liquor, may have his or her proportion of the annuities withheld from him or her for such time as the President may determine.

ARTICLE X. The United States further agree to guarantee the exclusive use of the reservation provided for in this treaty, as against any claims which may be urged by the Hudson Bay Company under the provisions of the treaty between the United States and Great Britain of the 15th of June, 1846, in consequence of the occupation of a trading post on the Pru-in River by the servants of that company.

ARTICLE XI. It is, moreover, provided that the Bitter Root Valley, above the Loo-lo Fork, shall be carefully surveyed and examined, and if it shall prove, in the judgment of the President, to be better adapted to the wants of the Flathead tribe than the general reservation provided for in this treaty, then such portions of it as may be necessary shall be set apart as a separate reservation for the said tribe. No portion of the Bitter Root Valley, above Loo-lo Fork, shall be opened to settlement until such examination is had and the decision of the President made known.

ARTICLE XII. This treaty shall be obligatory upon the contracting parties as soon as the same shall be ratified by the President and Senate of the United States.

1872 TREATY WITH CHARLO'S FORGED SIGNATURE

Articles of agreement made this 27th day of August, 1872, between James A. Garfield, special commissioner, authorized by the Secretary of the Interior to carry into execution the provisions of the act approved June 5, 1872, for the removal of the Flathead and other Indians from the Bitter Root Valley, of the first part, and Charlot, first chief, Arlee, second chief, and Adolf, third chief, of the Flatheads, of the second part, witnesseth:

Whereas it was provided in the eleventh article of the treaty concluded at Hell Gate July 16, 1855, and approved by the Senate March 8, 1859, between the United States and the Flatheads, Kootenay and Pend d'Oreille Indians, that the President shall cause the Bitter Root Valley above the Lo-Lo Fork to be surveyed and examined, and if, in his judgment, it should be found better adapted to the wants of the Flathead tribe, as a reservation for said tribe, it should be so set apart and reserved; and whereas the President did, on the 14th day of November, 1871, issue his order setting forth that "the Bitter Root Valley had been carefully surveyed and examined in accordance with said treaty," and did declare that "it is therefore ordered that all Indians residing in said Bitter Root Valley be removed as soon as practicable to the Jocko Reservation, and that a just compensation be made for improvements made by them in the Bitter Root Valley; and whereas the act of Congress above ·ecited, approved June 5, 1872, makes provision for such compensation: Therefore,

It is hereby agreed and covenanted by the parties to this instrument:

First. That the party of the first part shall cause to be erected sixty good and substantial houses, twelve feet by sixteen each, if so large a number shall be needed for the accommodation of the tribe; three of ˄aid houses, for the first, second, and third chiefs of said tribe, to be of double the size mentioned above; said houses to be placed in such portion of the Jocko Reservation, not already occupied by other Indians, as said chiefs may select.

Second. That the superintendent of Indian affairs for Montana Territory shall cause to be delivered to said Indians 600 bushels of wheat, the same to be groun·l into flour without cost to said Indians, and delivered to them in good condition during the first year after their removal, together with such potatoes and other vegetables as can be spared from the agency farm.

Third. That said superintendent shall, as soon as practicable, cause suitable portions of land to be inclosed and broken up for said Indians, and shall furnish them with a sufficient number of agricultural implements for the cultivation of their grounds.

Fourth. That in carrying out the foregoing agreement as much as possible shall be done at the agency by the employés of the Government; and none of such labor or materials, or provisions furnished from the agency, shall be charged as money.

Fifth. The whole of the $5,000 in money. now in the hands of the said superintendent, appropriated for the removal of said Indians, shall be paid to them in such form as their chiefs shall determine, except such portion as is necessarily expended in carrying out the preceding provisions of this agreement.

Sixth. That there shall be paid to said tribe of Flathead Indians the further sum of $50,000, as provided in the second section of the act above recited, to be paid in ten annual installments, in such manner and material as the President may direct; and no part of the payments herein promised shall in any way affect or modify the full right of said Indians to the payments and annuities now and hereafter due them under existing treaties.

Seventh. It is understood and agreed that this contract shall in no way interfere with the rights of any member of the Flathead tribe to take land in the Bitter Root Valley under the third section of the act above cited.

Eighth. And the party of the second part hereby agree and promise that when the houses have been built as provided in the first clause of this agreement they will remove the Flathead tribe to said houses (except such as shall take land in the Bitter Root Valley), in accordance with the third section of the act above cited, and will thereafter occupy the Jocko Reservation as their permanent home. But nothing in this agreement shall deprive said Indians of their full right to hunt and fish in any Indian country where they are now entitled to hunt and fish under existing treaties. Nor shall anything in this agreement be so construed as to deprive any of said Indians, so removing to the Jocko Reservation, from selling all their improvements in the Bitter Root Valley.

JAMES A. GARFIELD,
Special Commissioner for the Removal of the Flatheads
from the Bitter Root Valley.
CHARLOT, his x mark,
First Chief of the Flatheads.
ARLEE, his x mark,
Second Chief of the Flatheads.
ADOLF, his x mark,
Third Chief of the Flatheads.

126

1877 CANADIAN TREATY NUMBER SEVEN

Report of meeting between representatives of the Queen and representatives of the Blood, Piegan, and Sarcee tribes of Indians, the first meeting being held at Fort Mcleod on October 16, 1877.

PIEGAN CHIEF -"My children (the North Peigans) have looked long for the arrival of the Great Mother's Chief; one day we did not look for him, and he passed us; we have travelled after him for fourteen nights, and now are glad to see and shake hands with the Great Chief."

BEAR'S PAW (Stoney Chief) - "We have been watching for you for many moons now, and a long time has gone by since I and my children first heard of your coming. Our hearts are now glad to see the Chief of the Great Mother, and to receive flour and meat and anything you may give us. We are of one mind, and will say what we think on Wednesday."

SECOND DAY

Lieut.-Gov. Laird:

"The Great Spirit has made all things - the sun, the moon, and the stars, the earth, the forests, and the swift running rivers. It is by the Great Spirit that the Queen rules over this great country and other countries. The Great Spirit has made the white man and the red man brothers, and we should take each other by the hand. The Great Mother loves all her children, white man and red man alike; she wishes to do them all good. The bad white man and the bad Indian she alone does not love, and them she punishes for their wickedness. The good Indian has nothing to fear from the Queen or her officers. You Indians know this to be true. When bad white men brought you whiskey, robbed you, and made you poor, and, through whiskey, quarrel amongst yourselves, she sent the Police to put an end to it. You know how they stopped this and punished the offenders, and how much good this has done. I have to tell you how much pleased the Queen is that you have taken the Police by the hand and helped them, and obeyed her laws. The great Mother heard that the buffalo were being killed very fast, and to prevent them from being destroyed her Councillors have made a law to protect them. This law is for your good. It says that the calves are not to be killed in winter or spring, excepting by the Indians when they are in need of them as food. This will save the buffalo, and provide you with food for many years yet, and it shows you that the Queen and her Councillors wish you well.

Many years ago our Great Mother made a treaty with the Indians far away by the great waters in the east. A few years ago she made a treaty with those beyond the Touchwood Hills and the Woody Mountains. Last year a treaty was made with the Crees along the Saskatchewan, and now the Queen has sent Col. Mcleod and myself to ask you to make a treaty. But in a very few years, the Buffalo will probably all be destroyed, and for this reason the Queen wishes to help you to live in the future in some other way. She wishes you to allow her white children to come and live on your land and raise cattle, and should you agree to this, she will assist you to raise cattle and grain, and thus give you the means of living when the buffalo are not more. She will also pay you and your children money every year, which you can spend as you please. By being paid in money you cannot be cheated, as with it you can buy what you may think proper.

The queen wishes us to offer you the same as was accepted by the Crees. I do not mean exactly the same terms, but equivalent terms, that will cost the Queen the same amount of money. Some of the other Indians wanted farming implements, but these you do not require, as your lands are more adapted to raising cattle, and cattle, perhaps, would be better for you. The Commissioners will give you your choice, whether cattle or farming implements. I have already said we will give you money. I will now tell you how much. If you sign the treaty every man, woman and child will get twelve dollars each; the money will be paid to the head of each family for himself, woman and children; every year forever, you, your women and your children will get five dollars each. This year Chiefs and Councillors will be paid a larger sum than this; Chiefs will get a suit of clothes, a silver medal, and a flag, and every third year will get another suit. A reserve of land will be set apart for you and your cattle, upon which none others will be permitted to encroach; for every five persons one square mile will be allotted on this reserve, on which they can cut the trees and brush for firewood and other purposes, the Queen's officers will permit no white man or Half-breed to build or cut the timber on your reserve. If required roads will be cut through them. Cattle will be given to you, and potatoes, the same as are grown at Fort Mcleod. The Commissioners would strongly advise the Indians to take cattle, as you understand cattle better than you will farming for some time, at least as long as you continue to move about in lodges.

Ammunition will be issued to you each year, and as soon as you sign the treaty one thousand five hundred dollars' worth will be distributed amongst the tribes, and as soon as you settle, teachers will be sent to you to instruct your children to read books like this one (the Governor referred to a Bible), which is impossible so long as you continue to move from place to place. I have now spoken. I have made you acquainted with the principal terms contained in the treaty which you are asked to sign.

You may wish time to talk it over in your council lodges; you may not know what to do before you speak your thoughts in council. Go, therefore, to your councils, and I hope that you may be able to give me an answer tomorrow. Before you leave I will hear your questions and explain any matter that may not appear clear to you."

THIRD DAY

Lieut.-Gov. Laird:

"I expect to listen to what you have to say today, but, first, I would explain that it is your privilege to hunt all over the prairies, and that should you desire to sell any portion of your land, or any coal or timber from off your reserves, the Government will see that you receive just and fair prices, and that you can rely on all the Queen's promises being fulfilled. Your payments will be punctually made. You all know the Police; you know that no promise of theirs to you has ever been broken; they speak and act straight. You have perfect confidence in them, and by the past conduct of the Police towards you, you can judge of the future. I think I have now said all, and will listen to you and explain anything you wish to know; we wish to keep nothing back."

BUTTON CHIEF - "The Great Spirit sent the white man across the great waters to carry out His (the Great Spirit's) ends. The Great Spirit, and not the Great Mother, gave us this land. The Great Mother sent Stamixotokon (Col. McLeod) and the Police to put an end to the traffic in fire-water. I can sleep now safely. Before the arrival of the Police, when I laid my head down at night, every sound frightened me; my sleep was broken; now I can sleep sound and am not afraid. The Great Mother sent you to this country and we hope she will be good to us for many years. I hope and expect to get plenty; we think we will not get so much as the Indians receive from the Americans on the other side; they get large presents of flour, sugar, tea, and blankets. The Americans gave at first large bags of flour, sugar and many blankets; the next year it was only half the quantity, and the following years it grew less and less, and now they give only a handful of flour. We want to get fifty dollars for the Chiefs and thirty dollars each for all the others, men, women and children, and we want the same every year for the future. We want to be paid for all the timber that the Police and whites have used since they first came to our country. If it continues to be used as it is, there will soon be no firewood left for the Indians. I hope, Great Father, that you will give us all this that we ask."

CROWFOOT - "Great Father, what do you think now, what do you say to that? What I have to say will be spoken tomorrow. My brother Chiefs will speak now."

EAGLE TAIL - "Great Father, from our Great Mother, Stamixotokon and officers of the Police, the advise and help I received from the Police I shall never forget as long as the moon brightens the night, as long as water runs and the grass grows in spring, and I expect to get the same from our Great Mother. I hope she will supply us with flour, tea, tobacco and cattle, seed and farming implements. I have done at present."

OLD SUN - "Father and sons, I shall speak tomorrow."

GOVERNOR - "I fear Button Chief is asking too much. He has told us of the great good the Police have done for him and his tribe and throughout the country by driving away the whiskey traders, and now he wants us to pay him for the timber that has been used. Why, you Indians ought to pay us rather, for sending these traders in fire water away and giving you security and peace, rather than we pay you for the timber used. (Here the Indians indulged in a general hearty laugh at the proposition.) We cannot do you good and pay you too for our protection. Button Chief wants us to prevent the Crees and Half-Breeds from coming in and killing the buffalo. They too are the Queen's children, as well as the Blackfeet and Crees. We have done all we can do in preventing the slaying of the young buffalo, and this law will preserve the buffalo for many years. Button Chief wishes to get the same every year as this year; this we cannot promise. We cannot make a treaty with you every year. We will give you something to eat each year, but not so much as you will receive now. He says that Americans at first gave the Indians many large sacks fo flour, and now they only receive a handful. From us you will receive money to purchase what you may see fit, and as your children increase yearly, you will get the more money in the future, as you are paid so much per head.

(To the Stoney Chiefs) - When your reserves will be allotted to you no wood can be cut or be permitted to be taken away from them without your own consent. The reserve will be given to you without depriving you of the privilege to hunt over the plains until the land be taken up.

THE TREATY WITH THE BLACKFEET, NUMBER SEVEN

ARTICLES OF A TREATY made and concluded this twenty-second day of September, in the year of our Lord one thousand eight hundred and seventy-seven, between Her Most Gracious Majesty the Queen of Great Britain and Ireland, by her Commissioners, the Honorable David Laird, Lieutenant-Governor and Indian Superintendent of the North-West Territories, and James Farquharson McLeod, C.MG., Commissioner of the States boundary line, east of the central range of the Rocky Mountains, and south and west of Treaties Number Six and Four, by their head Chiefs and minor Chiefs or Councillors, chosen as hereinafter mentioned, of the other part:

WHEREAS the Indians inhabited the said territories, have pursuant to an appointment made by the said Commissioners, been convened at a meeting of the "Blackfoot Crossing" of the Bow River, to deliberate upon certain matters of interest to Her Most Gracious Majesty, of the one part, and the said Indians of the other;

AND WHEREAS the said Indians have been informed by Her Majesty's Commissioners that it is the desire of Her Majesty to open up for settlement, and such other purposes as to Her Majesty may seem meet, a tract of country, bounded and described as hereinafter mentioned, and to obtain the consent thereto of her Indian subjects inhabiting the said tract, and to make a treaty, and to arrange with them, so that there may be peace and good will between them and Her Majesty, and between them and Her Majesty's other people subjects; and that her Indian people may know and feel assured of what allowance they are to count upon and receive from Her Majesty's bounty and benevolence:

AND WHEREAS the Indians of the said tract, duly convened in council, and being requested by Her Majesty's Commissioners to present their head Chiefs and minor Chiefs, or Councillors, who shall be authorized, on their behalf, to conduct such negotiations and sign any treaty to be founded thereon, and to become responsible to Her Majesty for the faithful performance by their respective bands of such obligations as should be assumed by them, the said Blackfeet, blood, Piegan and Sarcee Indians have therefore acknowledged for that purpose, the several head and minor Chiefs, and the said Stoney Indian, the Chiefs and the Councillors who have subscribed hereto, that thereupon in open council the said Commissioners received and acknowledged the head and minor Chiefs and the Chiefs and Councillors presented for the purpose aforesaid:

AND WHEREAS the said Commissioners have proceeded to negotiate a treaty with the said Indians; and the same has been finally agreed upon and concluded as follows, that is to say: the Blackfeet, Blood, Peigan, Sarcee, Stony and Stony Indians inhabiting the district hereinafter more fully described and defined, do hereby cede, release, surrender and yield up to the Government of Canada for Her Majesty the Queen and her surrender and yield up to the Government of Canada for Her Majesty the Queen and her successors forever, all their rights, titles and privileges whatsoever to the lands included within the following limits, that is to say:

Commencing at a point on the international boundary due south of the western extremity of the Cypress Hills: thence west along the said boundary to the central range of the Rocky Mountains, or to the boundary of the Province of British Columbia; thence north-westerly along the said boundary to a point due west of the source of the main branch of the Red Deer River; thence south-westerly and southerly following on the boundaries of the tracts ceded by the Treaties Number Six and Four to the place of commencement, and also all their rights, titles and privileges whatsoever, to all other lands wherever situated in the North-West Territories, or in any other portions of the Dominion of Canada;

129

To have and to hold the same to Her Majesty the Queen and her successors forever;

And Her Majesty the Queen hereby agrees with her said Indians, that they shall have right to pursue their vocations of hunting throughout the tract surrendered as heretofore described, subject to such regulations as may, from time to time, be made by the Government of the country, acting under the authority of Her Majesty; and saving and excepting such tracts as may be required or taken up from time to time for settlement, mining, trading or other purposes by her Government of Canada, or by any of her Majesty's subjects duly authorized therefore by the said Government.

It is also agreed between Her Majesty and her said Indians that reserves shall be assigned them of sufficient area to allow one square mile for each family of five persons, or in that proportion for larger and smaller families, and that said reserves shall be located as follows, that is to say:

First, — The reserves of the Blackfeet, Blood and Sarcee bands of Indians, shall consist of a belt of land on the north side of the Bow and South Saskatchewan Rivers, of an average width of four miles along said rivers, downstream, commencing at a point on the Bow River twenty miles north-westerly of the "Blackfoot Crossing" thereof, and extending to the Red Deer River at its junction with the South Saskatchewan: also for the term of ten years, and no longer, from the date of the concluding of this treaty, when it shall cease to be a portion of said Indian reserves, as fully to all intents and purposes as if it had not at any time been included therein, and without any compensation to individual Indians for improvements, of a similar bolt of land on the south side of the Bow and Saskatchewan Rivers of an average width of one mile along said rivers, down stream; commencing as the aforesaid point on the seam on said river, about five miles below the said "Blackfoot Crossing." Beginning again one mile east of the said coal seam and extending to the Maple Creek mouth at its junction with the South Saskatchewan; and beginning again at the junction of the Bow River with the latter river, and extending on both sides of the South Saskatchewan in an average width on each side thereof of one mile, along said river against the stream, to the junction of the Little Bow River with the latter river, reserving to Her Majesty, as may now or hereafter be required by her for the use of her Indian and other subjects, from all the reserves hereinbefore described, the right to navigate the above mentioned rivers, to build bridges and establish ferries thereon, to use the farms thereof and all the trails leading thereto, and to open such other roads through the said reserves as may appear to Her Majesty's Government of Canada, necessary for the ordinary travel of her Indian and other subjects, due compensation being paid to individual Indians for improvements, when the same may be in any manner encroached upon by such roads.

Secondly — That the reserve of the Piegan band of Indians shall be on the Old Man's River, near the foot of the Porcupine Hills, at a place called Crow's Creek."

And thirdly — the reserve of the Stony band of Indians shall be in the vicinity of Morleyville.

In view of the satisfaction of Her Majesty with the recent general good conduct of her said Indians, and in extinguishment of all their past claims, she hereby, through her Commissioners, agrees to make them a present payment of twelve dollars each in cash to each man, woman and child of the families here represented.

Her Majesty also agrees that next year, and annually afterwards forever, she will cause to be paid to the said Indians, in cash, at suitable places and dates, of which the said Indians shall be duly notified, to each Chief, twenty-five dollars, each minor Chief or Councillor (not exceeding fifteen minor Chiefs to the Blackfeet and Blood Indians, and four to the Piegan and Sarcee bands, and five Councillors to the Stony Indian Bands) fifteen dollars, and to every other Indian of whatever age, five dollars; the same, unless there be some exceptional reason, to be paid to the heads of families for those belonging thereto.

Further, Her Majesty agrees that the sum of two thousand dollars shall hereafter every year be extended in the purchase of ammunition for distribution among the said Indians; provided that if at any future time ammunition became comparatively unnecessary for said Indians, her Government, with the consent of said Indians, or any of the bands thereof, may expend the proportion due to such band otherwise for their benefit.

130

Further , Her Majesty agrees that each head Chief and minor Chief, and each Chief and Councillor duly recognized as such, shall, once in every three years, during the term of their office, receive a suitable suit of clothing, and each head Chief and Stony Chief, in recognition of the closing of the treaty, a suitable metal and flag, and next year, or as soon as convenient, each head Chief, and minor Chief, and Stony Chief shall receive a Winchester rifle.

Further, Her Majesty agrees to pay the salary of such teachers to instruct the children of said Indians as to her Government may seem advisable, when said Indians are settled on their reserves and shall desire teachers.

Further, Her Majesty agrees to supply each head and minor Chief, and each Stony Chief, for the use of their bands, ten axes, five handsaws, five augers, one grindstone, and the necessary files and whetstones.

And further, Her Majesty agrees that the Indians shall be supplied as soon as convenient, after any band shall make due application therefore, with the following cattle for raising stock, that is to say: for every family of five persons, and under, two cows; for every family of more than five persons, and less than ten persons, three cows; for every family of over ten persons, four cows; and every head and minor Chief, for the use of their bands, one bull; but if any band desire to cultivate the soil as well as raise stock, each family of such band shall receive one cow less than the above mentioned number, and in lieu thereof, when settled on their reserves and prepared to break up the soil, two hoes, one spade, one scythe, and two hay forks, and for every three families, one plough and one harrow, and for each band, enough potatoes, barley, oats, and wheat (if such seeds be suited for the locality of their reserves) to plant the land actually broken up. All the aforesaid articles to be given, once and for all, for the encouragement of the practice of agriculture among the Indians.

And the undersigned Blackfeet, Blood, Piegan and Sarcee head Chiefs and minor Chiefs, and Stony Chiefs, and Councillors, on their own behalf and on behalf of all other Indians inhabiting the tract within ceded do hereby solemnly promise and engage to strictly observe this treaty, and also to conduct and behave themselves as good and loyal subjects of Her Majesty the Queen. They promise and engage that they will, in all respects, obey and abide by the law, that they will maintain peace and good order between themselves and other tribes of Indians, and between breeds or whites, now inhabiting, or hereafter to inhabit, any part of the said ceded tract; and that they will not molest the person or property of any inhabitant of such ceded tract, or the property of Her Majesty the Queen, or interfere with or trouble any person, passing or travelling through the said tract or any part thereof, and that they will assist the officers of Her Majesty in bringing to justice and punishment any Indian offending against the stipulations of this treaty, or infringing the laws in force in the country so ceded.

In witness whereof Her Majesty's said Commissioners, and the said Indian head and minor Chiefs, and Stony Chiefs and Councillors, have hereunto subscribed and set their hands, at the "Blackfoot Crossing" of the Bow River, the date and year herein first above written.

DAVID LAIRD
    Gov. of N.W.T. and Special Indian Commissioner.
JAMES F. McLEOD
    Lieut. - Colonel, Com. N.W.M.P., and Special Indian Comissioner
CHAPO-MEXICO
    (or Crowfoot), Head Chief of the South Blackfoot
NATOSE-APIW
    (or Old Sun, Head Chief of the North Blackfeet.
STAMIKSOTOCAR
    (or Bull Head), Head Chief of the Sarcees.
MEKASTO
    (or Red Crow)

NATOSE-ONISTA
(or Medicine Calf)
POKAPIW-OTOKAN
(or Bad Head)
SOTENAH
(or Rainy Chief), Head Chief of the North Bloods.
TAKOYO STAMIX
(or Friend Bull)
AKKA-KITCIPIMIW-OTAS
(or Many Spotted Horses)
ATSISTAH-MACAN
(or Running Rabbit)
PITAH-PEKIS
(or Eagle Rib)
SAKOYE-AOTAN
(or Heavy Shield), Head Chief of the Middle Blackfeet.
ZOATZE-TAPITAPIW
(or Setting on a Eagle Tail), Head Chief of the North Piegans.
AKKA-NAKKOYE
(or Many Swans)
APENAKO-SAPOP
(or Morning his Plume)

PITAH-ANNES
(or Eagle Robe)
STAMIX-OTA-KA-PIW
(or Bull Turn Round)
MASTE-PITAH
(or Crow Eagle)
JAMES DIXON
ABRAHAM KECHEPWOT
PATRICK KECHEPWOT
GEORGE MOY-ANY-MEN
GEORGE CRAWLER,
Stony Councillors.
EKAS-KINE
(or Low Horn)
KAYO-OKOSIS
(or Bear Shield)
PONOKAH-STAMIX
(or Bull Elk)
PITAH-SIKSINUM
(or White Eagle)
APAW-ONISTAW
(or Weasel Calf)

132

ATSISTA-HAES
(or Rabbit Carrier)
PITAH
(or Eagle)
PITAH ONISTAH
(or Eagle White Calf)
KAYE-TAPO
(or Going to Bear)

MAS-GWA-AH-SID
(or Bear's Paw)
CHE-NE-KA
(or John)
KI-CHI-PWOT
(or Jacob) Stony Chiefs
STAMIX-OSOK
(or Bull Bacfat)
EMITAH-APISKINNE
(or White Striped Dog)
MATAPI-KOMOTZIEW
(or the Captive or Stolen Person)
APAWAWAKSOW
(or White Antelope)
MAKOYE-KIN
(or Wolf Collar)
AYE-STIPIS-SIMAT
(or Heavily Whipped)
KISSOUM
(or Day Light)
PITAH-OTOCAN
(or Eagle Head)
APAW-STAMIX
(or Weasel Bull)
ONISTAh-POKAh
(or White Calf)
NETAH-KITEI-PI-MEW
(or Only Spot)
AKAK-OTOS
(or Many Horses)
STOKIMATIS
(or The Drum)
PITAH-OTSIKIN
(or Eagle Shoe)

ABOVE: Back near the treaty - signing days in a Blackfoot camp, when the presence of outsiders - like the mounted policeman in back, or the photographer - was still a notable event. Canadian Prairies, c. 1880. (C.W. Mathers Photo)

These fine Native American Books by native authors are available from
The Book Publishing Company
P.O. Box 99
Summertown, TN 38483

Basic Call to Consciousness	$7.95
Blackfoot Craftworkers' Book	11.95
Dreamfeather	9.95
Good Medicine: Life in Harmony with Nature	9.95
How Can One Sell the Air?	4.95
Indian Tribes of the Northern Rockies	9.95
Legends Told by the Old People	4.95
The People: Native American Thoughts and Feelings	5.95
Song of Seven Herbs	10.95
Spirit of the White Bison	5.95
Teachings of Nature	7.95
Traditional Dress	4.95

Please include $1.00 per book for shipping and handling.